W9-AUI-720

To Lydia, who makes the most sumptuous garden I know —
Valerie, Jordan & Jared

THE
sensuous
GARDEN

MONTAGU DON

THE
sensuous

SIMON &
SCHUSTER
EDITIONS

GARDEN

CONTENTS

INTRODUCTION

Sensuous gardening is easy. It happens. As sentient beings we have no choice in the matter. But unfortunately most of us stumble around in a state of frozen sensibility, too busy to feel, too focused on getting and achieving things to allow sensations to lead us wherever they might go, and too influenced by rationality to give them the importance they deserve.

Gardening has become a part of life in which control is paramount. Every aspect of the garden is under the rigid dictatorship of gardeners who nevertheless constantly complain about the "battle" they are waging against incipient disorder and engulfment by the wild forces of nature. We all do it. I found myself advising caution to someone wanting advice on converting their lawn into a flowering meadow. While applauding the notion I went on—to my subsequent shame—to describe at length the technical difficulties and careful control needed to get a proper fertility level and balance of species lest the "weeds" dominate the flowers. With hindsight I had taken a delightful concept and turned it on its head so that it became just another aspect of tight-lipped lawn maintenance.

We have to let go. This means accepting failure with a shrug of the shoulders and success with delight rather than with triumph. Our gardens are out there to be enjoyed, not conquered.

I suppose that the logical conclusion of this argument is to abandon gardening altogether and let the space it occupies do its own thing entirely, while we merely observe and enjoy it. I do not regard this as ridiculous but it denies the skill and artistry in gardening. I believe that it is possible to exercise one's talents in a controlled, careful fashion without denying the full flow of sensory pleasure. This is partly a matter of enjoying and using the happy accidents that inevitably happen when you experiment in the garden, rather than seeing them as failures that have to be eradicated in order to reach your predetermined goal.

Women tend to be very much better at this than men, although of course some women gardeners plan meticulously. But we all have both a masculine and feminine side to us and I suspect that every good male gardener is more in tune with his female nature than many men. It is a necessary skill (for it can be acquired) to enjoy any garden fully. It means being more haphazard in the planning and development of the garden, letting things happen, and reacting to them rather than determining everything in advance as though a garden design was a business plan. It means making the garden up as you go along, operating on different fronts at

OPPOSITE: *Horticultural reference informs us this is an agave, from which we usually dryly catalogue its growing habits instead of simply marveling at an astonishing piece of living sculpture.*

once as the mood takes you, doing little bits here and there all the time rather than projects and blitzes that are measurable like a battle campaign. The projects have to happen—indeed such enterprises as planning a herb garden, making a pond, or creating a shady spot in which to sit in summer are exciting and fun—but only as an exception to the rule. Sensuous gardening means noticing the emotions and responses you experience when you garden, and adapting the garden to encourage these feelings. If you feel good walking through woods then make a woods in the garden—even if it is only two trees together. It is enough to recreate that sensuous pleasure which woodland gives.

Of course we have to be open to the full range of sensory perception. For the most part we are unused to this, partly because too much sensation would overwhelm us and make daily life impossible and partly because sensations are like a muscle and if underused our ability to perceive them will shrink. To quote from Dr. John Collee writing in the London *Observer*:

"It is certain that our sensory powers, just like physical powers, can be trained and exercised to a level that seems supernatural. Consider the ability of winetasters to perceive precise flavors which are lost to the rest of us, or of the blind to 'read' street sounds like a map, or the deaf to lip-read by concentrating on the minutiae of facial expression."

He goes on to point out that "our senses are a) more sensitive than we would guess; b) more easily manipulated than we imagine; c) less objective than we would hope." Collee writes as a doctor who is primarily interested in the mechanics of sensation. How the senses work interests me less than observing and exploring the effects of their workings. My concern is to persuade people that gardening is a creative, sensuous activity offering a range of pleasures that go beyond almost any other human activity.

One of my pet hates is hearing people refer loftily to "real" gardeners as a mark of approval, as though there was such as thing as an unreal gardener. There is no level of skill or performance by which to establish your rank as a gardener. It is a completely egalitarian activity. Gardeners are people who garden. They do so privately, at home, often with people they love. It is an intimate thing without any external measure of value. The only thing to go by is how much pleasure both the garden itself and the process of making it gives you.

In the end the most interesting thing in any garden is the person who gardens it, and this book is not about plants or plans but about gardeners with feelings and sensations. And that is you.

OPPOSITE: *Maples provide the best of autumn color. It is important to let yourself respond to the thing itself rather than just learning why and how it comes about.*

TOUCH

The closest that we can get to any

garden is only skin deep.

Of all the senses, touch understands

least, knows most.

ABOVE: *These hairy, furrowed, frost-encrusted leaves belong to* Salvia argentea.
As a piece of tactile sculpture they are difficult to better.

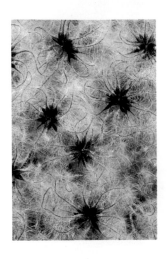

ABOVE: *Although both pictures are of seeds, the contrast between the knobbly compactness of one (Gunnera manicata) and the soft featheriness of the other (clematis) is enormous.*
OPPOSITE: *Moss on a woodland floor is a wall-to-wall velvet carpet between the trees.*

GARDENING WITHOUT TOUCH *is a relationship not consummated or made whole. This is not just an arch crossover from sensuous awareness to sensuality, but an awareness that the relationship between hand and garden is akin to that of lovers: be it the real passion and sweat of digging or planting a tree, or the casual hand that brushes a leaf in passing just as one lover brushes a crumb from the corner of the other's lips. Your hands work and give in the garden all the time and in return you receive unlimited sensuous pleasure. I certainly need to feel the soil, touch every leaf or flower, and love the feel of a well-balanced spade, rake, or hoe in the hand.*

The most prosaic horticulture demands regular handling until the moment of consumption. Apples are twisted gently on their stalks to see if they will come away and are therefore ripe, the tulip curves of a pear weighed in the heel of the hand to test but not bruise. The tips of fingers tentatively pluck at a grape and measure the give in a second of careless but incredibly finely tuned assessment. Strawberries are lifted heavily off the damp, slug-ridden soil and coddled with straw, and the furry skin of a peach, feeling so like the head of a newborn child, produces an almost reflexlike delicacy of stroking. We cup the heavy bloom of a rose in our hand, stem between two fingers, so that not only may we raise it to our nose, we may also feel its weight (and worth) in our hand.

Yet the gardener's hands are invariably calloused and swollen with labor, ingrained with soil within the epidermis despite endless scrubbing. It is impossible to garden effectively with long or painted nails, and cuts and abrasions are inevitable. They are extraordinarily tough working tools with a range of capabilities and sensitivities beyond any machine.

But the hands are not the organ of touch any more than is the soft skin inside the elbow. Touch differs from sight, scent, sound, and taste in that it has no specialized piece of equipment to measure and sense it. The entire skin—all 20 sq. ft. (2 sq. m) of it—works to feel for us and we can simultaneously prick our finger while brushing a petal against our cheek and feeling our shirt scratch at the neck and the sun hot on our brow and a dribble of sweat running down our back. The skin has about 200,000 receptors for cold and heat, 500,000 for touch and pressure, and another 3 million for pain's nerve endings.

The skin knows nothing but feels everything. The brain alone makes sense out of feeling, and every type of tactile sensation, be it pleasure, pain, itch, or measurement, has to travel, via neutral receptors, to the brain to be interpreted.

The intensity, duration, and location of the sensation is fed to the brain by different receptors in the skin. Vibration, for example, has its own specialized receptor, and might be regarded as a separate sense, as might the ability to feel heat or pain. But for the purposes of this book I shall deal with only one amalgamated sense of touch, the intimate contact between garden and gardener.

SOIL

An old way that farmers in the west of England and in parts of America judged whether their soil was ready for sowing in the spring was to go into the field, drop their pants, and sit bare-cheeked on the ground. If the earth felt warm to their buttocks it was ready; if not they would wait a while longer before sowing, regardless of sunshine or the calendar.

While this might seem extreme for the average back garden, the lesson has the essence of good soil management. The relationship between gardener and soil must always be intimate. It is not enough to maintain a detached, academic stance. You have to know your ground in all its humors and manifestations.

To love the soil, to luxuriate in it, is to try to know the thing that made you. There is something atavistically pure and unintellectual about planting a seed and seeing it grow. Something absurd, too, because we play little enough part in the process. But the absolute simplicity of working the soil—of seeing it become rich and crumbly, of feeling it flow like silk through one's fingers, or of reaching that state of germinating heaven when it can be squeezed to a fragile clod that holds in the hand but shatters when dropped back to the ground—that is a pure, sensual pleasure that does not need to be hidden behind technique. Soil is to the gardener's hands what air is to the wings of a bird. It is their medium and they must learn to feel it, to run it through their fingers and know in their skin when it is ready, just as a baker knows when his dough is ready to bake. I realize that it is not a conventionally glamorous aspect of gardening. Flowers are the thing, the ground as abstract to most people as the air we depend on.

But everything in the garden begins and ends in the soil. The more that I garden the more certain I am that the one factor that makes for great gardens is the amount of care lavished on the soil. However carefully you choose and cultivate your plants, they will only perform as well as the soil allows them to.

Your hands need no horticultural experience to know when soil feels right. If you rummage your fingers down into the ground they work easily and inevitably, mimicking the growth of roots in the weeks and months to come. We use the word "dirt" and "soil" to describe unwanted stains and filth, which is a calumny against the earth. I love the sensation of dry dirt coating my fingers, the residue of careful work that enables something to grow and live outside.

Different types of soil have very different tactile characteristics. Clay is always heavy in the hand, sticky and cold when wet, rock hard when dry. It is a demanding taskmaster, yet is the most fertile of all soils and if worked well it will, as an old farmer once told me, "break your back and your heart but

never your bank balance." Sandy soil is gritty stuff and slips through the fingers carelessly. The individual particles are up to a thousand times larger than those in clay, letting water drain easily and making it imperative to work in plenty of organic matter to bulk it out and guard its reserves more jealously. But sandy soil warms up fast in spring and never becomes waterlogged, making it ideal for strawberries, grass, asparagus, potatoes, and herbs. I was raised on chalky soil and all my tactile memories are based upon its thin, loose structure. Often the topsoil is only a few inches deep before the solid white chalk is reached. Flint is only found in chalk and I associate the razor edges of black flint with it, nicking unsuspecting flesh. Unlike sandy soil chalk can mix with clay to become horribly sticky— pale mud. It needs beefing up with manure to retain moisture when dry and allow decent drainage when wet.

Peat is flaky to feel, like crumbling tobacco through the hand. When wet— which is usually the case as it is extremely moisture-retentive—it is cold and dense, a half-tamed bog in the garden, chilling to the touch.

In the end we all reach for loam. This is a perfect mixture of clay, sand, and organic matter, often taking years of intensive cultivation, adding manure, compost, grit, and lime. But when you have it you have it; you do not need any analysis to tell you: it just feels right.

ABOVE: *Seed beans ready for planting. They feel almost liquid in their polished shininess, a handful of featherweight pebbles to push in the ground.*
OPPOSITE: *Hands are the gardener's reality. Hands carry the scars and ingrained stories of hours in the garden, reaching, shaping, and caressing both plants and soil, feeding the brain with a stream of equally subtle and brutal tactile messages.*

LEFT: *After a while gloves take on the character of the hands that habitually inhabit them. These sit like a discarded skin, scarred by wear and tear. While intimate and direct contact with your soil is often a pleasure, there are times when gloves provide much-needed protection.*

OPPOSITE: *Gardening tools are often very beautiful and there is great pleasure in using handtools that have evolved to do specific work, and enable the work and the worker and the tool to seamlessly merge into a rhythmic flow.*

TOOLS

The act of weighing an object in the hand is an extraordinarily subjective process. There is a "rightness" to weight that is inexplicable in any other terms than "feel." This manifests itself most noticeably with hand tools. Given the choice of ten identical spades, one will feel more "right" than the other nine for every individual—even though it is possible for all ten to choose a different spade. It is impossible to know if the differences in the weights and balance of each spade correspond with unique standards of rightness within each person or whether we all share a sensation of what feels good and simply measure it in different ways according to our own strength and height, experience and inclination. The important thing is that it is idiosyncratic and intimate. The size of an object carries illusions about its weight: two trowels of exactly the same weight will always feel different according to their size. The rule is that a larger object will always feel lighter than a smaller one of identical weight, because the sensation of weight is governed not just by touch but by a preconception of how heavy we think something ought to be. To this end we generally expect darker objects to be heavier than pale ones (because they are "lighter"?).

Our favorite tools are an extension of ourselves, almost reaching for the hand as we grasp them, and becoming a perfect marriage of function and form as they are used, the tools defining the activity that man and implement perform. In fact there is a way in which a tool almost molds itself to a particular hand, becoming as individual as a much-used pen nib—although I imagine that the actual wear on the wood of a handle is minuscule. When you have this ideal tool in your hand and you are using it well—which should feel effortless and natural—then the function itself becomes pure pleasure and it does not matter what is being dug or cut or hoed or what the conditions are. There is a zenlike flow between man and inanimate object that is perfect harmony. A flight of romantic fantasy? No: gritty, practical reality, experienced sooner or later by every gardener and one of the less honored and greatest pleasures of gardening.

FEET

A glamorous friend of mine often has dirt-ingrained feet on a summer's day because she loves gardening with bare feet. There are those who would consider this eccentric but it seems to me to be eminently sensible, maximizing the sensory experience of an ordinary garden activity.

While it is not obligatory to dabble your bare feet in the dirt to get the most out of your garden, it is a pity not to go barefoot at some time. To clump about stolidly in socks and shoes is to deprive yourself of one type of intimacy with your garden.

Walk on the lawn with bare feet and the grass, somewhere between moist slipperiness and almost abrasive dryness, will be experienced in a way that sight alone can never give you. Children understand this instinctively; but gardeners can lose this aspect of experience when they become too involved in practicing the mechanics of gardening. We might know the different techniques and machinery needed to prepare, sow, and maintain a fine lawn, a lawn for children to play on, a lawn for wet or dry soil, grass for an orchard and a wildflower meadow, but can we accurately summon up the different physical sensations and textures of each different grassy area?

And most middle-aged people are much more familiar with the weeding demands of different types of hard surface, be it paving, bricks, gravel, crushed bark, or cobbles, than the variation of texture that only walking on them with bare feet could tell them. Cobbles have a knobbly discomfort, bricks a curiously wide range of texture and level; crushed bark is predictably soft, almost furry, and the difference between sharp and rounded gravel becomes aggressively apparent!

In the northern hemisphere we get used to gardening in Wellington boots for half the year. Wrapped in rubber we move carelessly through mud and puddles, almost relishing them. In light shoes these would become obstacles to be avoided, not part of our gardening experience.

The shoes we wear are important. Most of us have gardening boots and lacing them on is like putting on soccer boots before a game: it focuses the attention. As they become battered and well worn, they become objects of great affection, their soles bearing the imprint of miles walked cutting the grass, buckets of sweat lost digging the kitchen garden, and the accumulated gentleness of plants firmed into the ground by exactly the right pressure of heel.

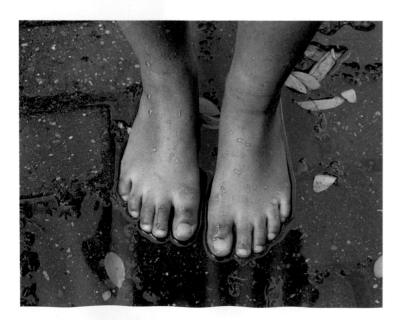

LEFT: *It should be compulsory for every gardener to walk barefoot in the garden at least once a month.*
OPPOSITE: *Digging is, among other things, a process of acquiring intimacy with your soil through the medium of your feet. It provides priceless information for the gardener.*

FOLIAGE

If you walk into the garden and close your eyes you quickly become aware of the importance of tactility in plants. An extraordinary range of textured leaves brush against you. Notice how your hands grasp and reach for surfaces unbidden, working as unselfconsciously as antennae. I know that as plants grow I have to add touch to the measurement of their progress, ruffling my hands through the anonymous leaves of daylilies months away from flowering or gently grazing the back of my hand with the featheriness of fennel (*Foeniculum vulgare*).

Some leaves are abrasive, but not aggressively so. I am thinking of the raised points on the elephantine leaves of *Gunnera manicata* that rasp across the skin. This roughness comes as a surprise (just as the coarse hair on the elephant's back is unexpected) on something that our eyes tell us should be soft and floppy. Our eyes may tell us that ferns are soft and delicate

things, unfurling from their green snail-like quills, but many ferns are curiously harsh to the touch. Take the fronds of *Blechnum chilense* and run them through your hands; they have a dry, reptilian texture. Horsetail (*Equisetum hyemale*) feels weird, although once you have touched it the plant remains in the memory longer as a tactile sensation than as a visual one, so it comes as no surprise. It is dry and harsh and strangely unpleasant. As it is one of the most pernicious weeds in the garden, I wish you ignorance of the dreadful stuff.

Shiny leaves invite rubbing—or polishing—and there is a spick-and-span quality to holly, camellias, laurel, and the buffed-up leaves of a houseproud rubber plant. The leaves of English holly (*Ilex aquifolium*) in spring are impossibly shiny and the temptation to touch and see if they are really as glistening wet as they seem is irresistible, year after year. American holly (*Ilex opaca*) is good for berries but lacks this varnished quality.

OPPOSITE: *Caught halfway through the process of clipping, the tight neatness of the sheared lavender balls makes a beautiful contrast with the spiky new growth of the plants yet to be trimmed.*

LEFT: *You must relish the perfect matte glaucous blue of the agave from a distance, for its leaves are as aggressively spiked as any plant.*

BELOW: *Frost on the leaves of* Meconopsis paniculata *adds to its unplantlike furriness.*

Furry-leafed plants like lamiums or *Stachys byzantina* positively invite you to stroke them, the downy covering of silver hairs almost caressing you back. I know that these hairs are there to trap moisture and reduce transpiration, thus making the plants suitable for dry conditions, but that is only a small part of my knowledge of the plant. Much more important is my awareness of how they will feel when I touch them, and that describes lamium on my mind map with a far greater depth of information, albeit knowledge that is wordless and too often undervalued.

Grasses often have the softness and tactility of hair. *Carex flagellifera* most fully fits this bill, but squirreltail grass (*Hordeum jubatum*), the Japanese *Hakonechloa macra* 'Aureola', and the rather taller shaggy *Helictotrichon sempervirens*, growing in glaucous clumps, are also grasses worth growing for feel alone.

Sometimes the senses work directly together. To release the fragrance of a scented-leaved pelargonium like 'Lady Plymouth', you have to coax the scent out with your fingers. The leaf is curiously dry to touch. Only when squeezed between thumb and forefinger does it give up its unseen sensual secret. So the hand learns to feel the smell as surely as the nose recognizes it.

It is not necessary to confine tactile experience to the hands. Take the fronds of fennel (*Foeniculum vulgare*) and brush your nose across the face of the flower.

Only then will its transience and fragility be brought home and its preciousness be underlined. This intimacy is direct, uncomplicated, and as important to your understanding of horticulture as any more practical piece of information. By the way, the end of the nose follows only fingertips and certain parts of the genitalia in the quantity of the receptors per square millimeter of skin.

Sometimes even the most delicate contact is resented by the plant. The leaves of the sensitive plant (*Mimosa pudica*) recoil from touch and send tiny electrical currents along the sap ducts to the base of each leaflet where it joins the stem. The cells there are filled with liquid which discharges on receiving this signal. Water from the leaves takes its place, causing the leaves to fold inward exactly like an umbrella. The whole operation takes about three seconds from the first contact. It will take another twenty minutes to refill their cells so that the leaves can open out into the sunlight.

ABOVE: *Color only tells part of the story. Texture refines and defines it. Stones are made animate by their velveteen covering of moss.*

BELOW (left to right): *The fanned ribs of a zantedeschia leaf resemble the patterns left by the tide on the wet sand of a beach, and the fluted stems of bamboo are like the polished bars of a cell. The unfurling, armadillo-like fronds of a fern hint at its coarseness of texture, and the giant leaves of a gunnera are as harsh and abrasive as elephant hide.*

BARK

Touch does not have to be gentle. The bark of a mature tree can be hugged, slapped, rasped, or even punched. Think of the range of barks available: shiny and smooth like the Tibetan cherry (*Prunus serrula*), which has irregular horizontal scars striping the most gleaming, rich, mahogany reddish brown bark; ridged in deep wrinkles like an oak; or soft and shredded like the thick bark of the wellingtonia (*Sequoiadendron giganteum*). I remember being told about the wellingtonia's softness and being unconvinced that such a massive tree could have—what seemed to my ten-year-old self—such an unlikely bark. So my father, an ex-boxer, stopped the car by the tree in question, stepped over the fence into some unwitting stranger's garden, and started to pummel the tree as hard as he could to prove his point. However, all the human anger in the world would make little impression on a tree whose bark grows to be 1 ft. (30 cm) thick or more.

The obvious purpose of bark is protection, especially from contact. Its effectiveness is vital to the survival of the plant, because the center of a tree is just dead wood. All the life takes place just

A mass of conflicting textural messages is given out by the sinuous roots of a yew tree growing over stone.

underneath the bark, in a band of cells that separates the bark from the wood. This is the green layer that contains the cambium which makes all new wood. Every year new wood cells are made on its inner side, causing the tree to thicken. These new cells are practically the sole source of sap to the new leaves growing each year. This means that the cambium also has to grow to match the internal girth of the trunk that it has created. On top of this it has to make phloem, the inner layer of bark, on its external circumference because that, too, increases year by year. Phloem is a spongy layer that provides a downward conduit for the sap as it carries sugar from the leaves (made by photosynthesis) to feed new wood cells as they are made, and to provide energy for the roots. As anyone that has had the misfortune to let horses into an orchard will know, it only takes the simple removal of a ring of this thin layer of cambium around the tree—any tree—to kill it. Only the bark separates this film-like layer of life from the potentially hostile outside world.

The west Himalayan birch (*Betula utilis* var. *jaquemontii*) looks its best by winter moonlight, glowing ghostlily. Like all birches it is constantly renewing its outer layers of bark. The paper birch (*B. papyrifera*) is perhaps the best of all white birches, its bark hanging off in delicious cream rolls like shot silk. It was fine enough for the Native Americans to use as paper and strong enough to make the hulls of their canoes.

The paper-bark maple (*Acer griseum*) is quite like a birch in the way that its bark peels. It is a small tree and the bark comes away in rich brown rags. Even the twigs peel, so that the whole tree is like a gorgeously eccentric russet dress.

These barks are extremely fragile. You cannot resist touching them, but only tentatively, aware that to do so is to destroy the thing that drew you to it. The peeling bark, of course, has had its day. The bark is peeling because the trunk is swelling beneath it and it is constantly renewed.

The Chinese stewartia (*Stewartia sinensis*) also has a thin bark, the top coat of which is a Pompeian red. It flays itself so that the ocher layer beneath can harden. Although the bark is thin and

papery, it has none of the preciousness of the maples or birches; the new skin is taut with readiness.

There is nothing fragile either about the muscularity of beech and hornbeam which you must feel with your hand—not your fingers, but the full palm of your hand—to appreciate it properly. Beneath the bark the tree is as bunched and coiled as a sprinter tensed for a race.

Some trees need no anthropomorphism to induce a bout of bark massage. In particular the Caucasian elm (*Zelkova carpinifolia*) develops cathedral-like buttresses on its trunk below branches that sprout dementedly like an inverted besom. A mature specimen is too large for just your hands and arms to do the work—a full body-to-trunk massage is called for if you are to get the full sensual experience (together with some very odd looks indeed from your neighbors). The Japanese zelkova (*Z. serrata*) has a much thinner bark, which flakes off to reveal a new, bright orange coat.

The bark of a young English elm (*Ulmus procera*) has a distinctive, almost cork-like texture. Unfortunately, it is only the young elms that we ever see now, as the trees are invariably killed by Dutch elm disease as they approach the age of twenty, which is when their bark becomes thick enough to house the beetle that causes the fungus. The American elm (*U. americana*) also suffers from the disease.

The field maple (*Acer campestre*) is another hedgerow tree with a texture that appears soft to the touch, although it has curious flanged "edges" to the stems which disappear after a few years. This tree, mercifully, seems to be free from disease.

One of my favorite barks is that of a mature pear tree. Sadly, this is becoming rare as fewer and fewer people grow standard fruit trees and all the old trees are cut down. As a pear matures the bark forms square platelets. If you trace your finger down the trunk it follows these in a gridlike maze, and because this pattern comes only with age, you suddenly become aware of the venerability of the tree, older than you, older than your parents, older, in all likelihood, than your grandparents.

Only the bark separates this filmlike layer of life

As some trees age, their barks develop appearances and textures that you would not suspect by looking at the young tree. The bark of the sweet chestnut (*Castanea sativa*) takes on a spiral pattern which, on ancient trees hundreds of years old, runs around the trunk in a deeply lined whirl. Tracing this with your hands takes you up the tree deviously, the form of the bark leading your hand astray. So strong are the ridges that it is hard to slide the palm of the hand up and down as instinct dictates. The horse chestnut (*Aesculus hippocastanum*) does not share this characteristic—but there is no reason why it should, as the two trees are entirely unrelated.

Most of the pines have textured bark, often beautifully colored, but my favorite is the Corsican pine (*Pinus nigra laricio*), which has black fissures lacing the trunk with ridges of ocher,

from the potentially hostile outside world.

pink, and gray. The texture of this lovely palette is rugged to the point of abrasion and makes a wonderfully contrasting combination with the delicacy of color.

Not all bark feels good. If you were to lift the outer layers of the bark of the slippery elm (*Ulmus rubra*), your fingers would encounter the mucilaginous surface that gives the tree its name. And your fingers would not like it.

FROM LEFT TO RIGHT: *The barks of the pear* (Pyrus communis)*, snow gum (*Eucalyptus pauciflora)*, London plane (*Platanus x hispanica)*, oak (*Quercus robusta)*, paper-bark maple (*Acer griseum)*, and* Acer rufinerve.

NOLI ME TANGERE

While most plants positively invite touch, there are those that have evolved means of defending themselves against it. So most roses are barbed with thorns, ranging from the enormous finlike spikes of *Rosa sericea pteracantha* to the hairy bristles of *R. pimpinellifolia*.

The contrast between a voluptuous flower and its thorn is curiously satisfying, as if there were a human need for a visible dichotomy between the spike and the bloom, making the latter seem all the more precious and desirable. But there has to be a balance in favor of beauty. Brambles are too much thorn and not enough flower. A stinging nettle in flower is a pretty thing and butterflies love them, but there is no gardener who does not curse nettles as hands throb and tingle half the night after being stung. Thistles of all kinds are beautiful, but the thorns act like splinters, often sneaking into your flesh unnoticed but needing extravagant excavation to extract them and causing nagging hurt until removed.

Some plants openly display their aggression like a cornered street fighter. No one comes off better in a brush with any cactus, holly, yucca, spear grass, or prickly pear. Other plants hurt with stealth. Neither giant hogweed (*Heracleum mantegazzianum*) nor rue (*Ruta graveolens*) has obvious stings or barbs, but the slightest brush with the leaves of either plant on skin that is exposed to intense ultraviolet rays causes painful blisters that take a long time to heal. The skin of the hands is usually tough enough to resist this, but never garden near either plant with your shirt off on a sunny day.

In North America poison ivy (*Toxicodendron radicans*) causes a nasty rash to those irresistibly drawn to touch it and some people do find themselves irritated by the milky sap of a number of euphorbias, although simple contact with the plants will do no harm.

Pain is a very intimate perception. It exists without any external indication. There can be phantom scents, hallucinations, sounds in the ear that do not exist, and uncalled-for tastes in the mouth, but pain always exists, although it is unrelated to the severity of the cause. A tiny thistle splinter can make the slightest contact intolerable, yet a deathly tumor can cause only a slight headache. Pain forewarns and modifies our behavior in a way that no other sensation (other than perhaps thirst and hunger) can do. In this way plants scare us off with a dose of pain—the sting is a threat rather than a punishment.

Of course plants are not the only dangers for the gardening hand. You will be constantly cut by stones; blistered and calloused by the fray of tools; your nails will be caught and ripped; your knuckles grazed. But the deepest cut will heal, the scars fading without the delicacy of touch diminishing.

Texture can work as the first line of defense, as in the thorny stems of brambles and roses. Primarily designed to stop the plant from being munched by grazing animals, the visual warning also keeps human hands away.

SIGHT

To see the world as a child sees it, or

as Van Gogh or William Blake saw it,

we must be prepared to unlearn, to let

go of the baggage of knowledge and

respond to instinct.

ABOVE: *Each individual flowerhead of* Agapanthus campanulatus *'Isis' is a rocketburst of violet hanging in an explosion of color.*

ABOVE: *Shape made with color. Purple campanulas are starkly outlined against a yellow background (top). The coiled structure of a box topiary is clearly defined by snow (bottom).*
OPPOSITE: *A doorway or gap in a wall or hedge will make sudden openings of light as well as vision. Here the shade acts as powerfully as the objects that are shaded.*

THE EYE MAKES NO ATTEMPT TO PERCEIVE WHAT IT SEES. *The brain, when it is up to it, does that. The eye feeds the brain a series of upside-down images split into left and right halves. These are inverted and superimposed to form one right-way-up picture. One rarely notices the process. I remember coming around from a major operation when I was ten, though. As I rose to a cloudy consciousness I became aware that the world had turned upside down. The nurses and the other beds were hanging from the ceiling and the lights stood up from the floor. I now know that my brain was too fluffy from the anesthetic to do its customary job of flipping over the received pictures. If I had been coming around from a sight-restoring operation after a lifetime of blindness, I would presumably have been unaware of the topsy-turvy nature of the images. Only experience had made the world have a "right" way up at all.*

Our eyes merely feed in a stream of images made up by light and pigment, which become shaped by habit, experience, and emotion. To respond to the raw sensuality of sight is difficult because there is so much information in the way. To see the world as a child sees it, or as Van Gogh or William Blake saw it, we must be prepared to unlearn, to let go of the baggage of knowledge and respond to instinct. It is very hard. We must learn to be empty in order to make room for pure sensation. How you react to this will always be personal and therefore fresh and new. You have to abandon some of the preoccupations of the busy gardener and give yourself the opportunity to recapture some perceptual innocence, enjoying images for what they appear to be rather than for what they mean.

Sight dominates our perception of any garden. We think of this as being an awareness of color, but it is a mixture of light, color, form, and contrast. Out of this we hunt for color. Even a "monochromatic" green garden has dozens of shades of green, ranging from almost blue to almost yellow, as well as the brown of the soil, the shades of the sky, sun, reflected light, material objects, paths, buildings—every garden is a swathe of color. On the whole we work at this and deliberately try to cram in as varied a palette as we can—often to chaotic effect.

The color wheel is an attempt to organize hues, demonstrating their relationships within the spectrum. It is helpful but not infallible. Yellows are easy to separate and classify as they move toward red, but as reds turn to blue, the distinctions between purple, violet, mauve, lilac, and lavender become muddy and inconclusive. The wheel also provides a starting point for understanding color combinations. Colors that are adjacent or close to each other, like red and orange or blue and violet, are known as harmonious colors; those that are on the opposite side, like yellow and blue, are contrasting colors. Colors that lie directly opposite, like blue and orange, are complementaries, and create the most vibrant contrasts. As with all rules, however, the color wheel takes us only so far. In the end, color combinations come down to our own personal preferences, which we must discover through observation and experiment.

Spring is crystalline, the light delicate yet as confident as birdsong.

LIGHT

Without light there is no color. Gardens are hardly ever without some light, be it from the moon, stars, or reflected light from houses, even streetlamps, or distant towns. But there is a lot less of it at night. Dark swallows up a garden teasingly, the dance of a thousand shrouds, edges dissolving, shade merging into shade until only the junction of garden and sky remains. Color clings precariously as light seeps away: a pale lily, white snowdrops under the trees, philadelphus bobbles across the spring darkness.

Moonlight is often enough to garden by, the place stripped of color, monochromatic under a cold white light. This is the nearest we have to black and white vision and it is good to look at your garden like this, because it simplifies shapes and forms,

highlighting certain aspects that are lost under the welter of normal color and hiding other things that shriek during the day. It also makes us realize how important certain pigments and tones are in achieving an emotional and sensual response.

You need to know your garden in all lights and aspects as part of your intimacy with it. At first you must seek this familiarity out, making the effort to see where the first light falls in midwinter compared to the midsummer dawn, seeing where the shade is deepest at the summer solstice, knowing that this area will be dramatically larger six months later.

The most constant factor of light in northern gardens is that it changes all the time. Morning light pitches across the garden from the east, almost horizontal at first, clear, even surprisingly

harsh over short distances, although hazy as sight nears the horizon. As the sun rises shadows shrivel, and we think of this as the "best" light of the day. There is certainly a lot of it on a cloudless day, but it is not the best light by which to see. For that you need to wait until the sun slopes down a little. On the Equator this happens at a tumble, the sun dropping in a hurry. One of the beauties of summer is that the sun leaves the sky only reluctantly, edging out with a swelling glow and the resulting light falls on the garden—a gift at the end of a beautiful day. All bright colors look better in the evening: reds, purples, and orange glowing from the shadows.

The seasons each have their own idiosyncratic qualities of light. Spring is crystalline, the light delicate yet as confident as birdsong. Summer is full-frontal glare; even cloud cover fails to dim its brightness. Autumnal light belongs to the leaves, shining softly like a lamp. Winter is worst. At best the gray light is pearly, but there are days that simply have to be endured, when all light seems sucked out of objects and the grayness hangs like a shroud over the tatters of plants. But there are compensations of the season, such as mornings of hoar frost when the tips of ice-wrapped branches shine with a pink glow and the astonishing clarity of snowy ground under radiant blue skies that no amount of summer sunshine can ever replicate, as well as the isolated shafts of sunlight that light up a single precious flower for a moment, bejeweling an entire day.

OPPOSITE: *Light is diffused and spangled by filtering leaves, but the contrasts are still sharp.*
ABOVE: *Dawn light on a midwinter's day is traced in the frost, proving that a flowerless garden in "bad" weather can still be breathtakingly beautiful.*

SHADE

Gardeners have an obsession with shade. Libraries are filled with books on plants for shade and techniques for getting the most out of what is generally assumed to be a profound disadvantage. While there is a deep psychological hunger for light, it seems curious that shade should be treated as an anomaly, a piece of bad luck that we have to cope with as best we can. After all, what we mean by shade is simply the effect of an object blocking the light source.

Shade is part of every garden and in many gardens its absence is the biggest problem, because very few plants thrive in unbroken sunlight. So the first thing to do is to abandon the convention that shade is a limitation on your gardening ambitions and see it as being as essential and natural as rain. It is a positive element of the garden and should be used to full advantage, not just to grow the plants that have naturally evolved to flourish in it but also as a visual respite from the sun. In midsummer every garden needs a shady spot where you can sit and eat, and this is best created by means of a screen from the sun rather than made from a site where the sun does not reach. This kind of shade wants to be a delicious pool, not a cold, dark pond.

From the deep gloom lurking in the lee of a high wall, where only a select (often interesting and beautiful) band of plants do well, to dappled light, shade

7:30 A.M.

10:00 A.M.

varies enormously. All woodland plants have evolved to make the most of shade, sometimes in a very sophisticated manner. Plants evolve to adapt to change. Primroses, wood sorrel, bluebells, and violets all thrive best in the half-shade of a shrub thicket. They flower in early spring when the light is only partly blocked by the bare branches, before the canopy has come into leaf.

2:30 P.M.

8:00 P.M.

Some colors stand out in shade better than others and it makes sense to use your armory of color to work with this rather than struggling against it. White is the easiest color to see in surrounding gloom and therefore will attract pollinators. In the harsh, unshaded light of midday white flowers are lost in the whiteness of the light. Blue is at its clearest when seen in shade. Dark does not diffuse it but makes it seem cooler to the eye. The "hot" colors—red, orange, bright yellow—are toned down by shade and paled by sun. They are best planted where they will receive low evening sunlight.

The garden is rich with a range of shaded light from spangles of a shadow cast by the end of a branch to the sharp-edged dark falling behind a solid object. It all adds dimension and texture to what would otherwise be a desert of unbroken light. A garden with no shade might grow a huge range of sun-loving plants, but it would be a dull place, sensuously barren.

Four photographs taken from the same spot at different times of day show how changing light alters our perception of the garden. The first, taken at 7:30 A.M., and the last, at 8 P.M., are the most photogenic, casting longer, softer shadows and drawing light from within the plants. The pictures taken at 10 A.M. and 2.30 P.M. have a harsher brightness with deeper shadows and a less flattering light. For this reason gardens always look better at dawn or dusk than in the middle of the day.

We can apply this principle to the garden, manipulating shade by pruning taller plants to allow more light into the base of a border, wall, or under a tree. We can also choose plants to make the most of the different levels of shade in each season. It is ironic that the season of brightest light—summer—is also the time of deepest shade, as there are so many leaves to create a barrier for the sunlight.

BROWN

Brown is a house with many mansions. Tan, bronze, roan, cinnamon, copper, coffee, chocolate, amber, umber, auburn, hazel, chestnut; these are all recognizably browns that do not individually define brown. They all have different connotations that evoke powerful separate responses. On the whole they are complimentary in a way that straight "brown" is not. How much more flattering it is to have hair described as auburn than as brown! But all shades of brown imply richness and depth. A washed-out, sepia tint or a dull ocher falls outside the range of a bona fide brown and edges toward yellow along with ochers.

The three primary colors produce brown and it is strange that red and green, the most violent and clear of companions, should mix to such muddy anonymity. Gardeners take brown for granted. It is there, unnoticed, unconsidered as a color. Yet, after green, it is by far the predominant hue in our vision at any one time, and from midwinter through to late spring it even overwhelms green, with brown bark, twigs, and above all, brown soil. All plant material returns to brown. Compost and soil, dust to dust, all the colors reduce down to a brown essence.

We expect earth to be brown. It sometimes isn't, scanning from black, gray, red, to yellow. Nevertheless, it meets that expectation more often than not. Most tool handles are the brown of formerly pale ash wood stained with dirty hands. Dress a gardener to stereotype and most will clothe him in heavy brown corduroy, cloth that most exactly mimics a freshly raked tilth.

Every autumn the fireburst of color from the dying leaves ends in brown. I love those leaves that remain long after the others have fallen: beech, hornbeam, and for a surprisingly long time, oak. My garden has over half a mile of hornbeam hedging and the leaves of milky coffee last through to spring until they are eventually replaced by a new generation of startling green. Exmoor, in southwestern England, is furnished throughout winter by gloriously russet beech hedges, mile upon mile of richness in a wild upland landscape. Another autumnal brown is provided by the distinctive fruits of the horse chestnut, which lie like brown marbles at the base of the tree, surrounded by tawny leaves, as shiny as a soldier's boots.

Brown flowers are a bit thin on the ground. Like green petals, one instinctively feels that they are a curiosity and perhaps too much of a good thing. But those that do exist are wonderful, imbued with a velvety lushness inherent from their red ancestry. Sunflowers instantly evoke a solar yellowness, yet they come in gloriously rich browns (and oranges) as well. *Helianthus* 'Velvet Queen' is as good as any. *Helleborus orientalis* comes in many dark shades; some, like *H.o.* 'Philip Ballard' are a deep, plum-tinged brown. *Rudbeckia hirta* 'Nutmeg' is so named because it is brown(ish). There is no "ishness" about *Iris* 'Witch of Endor'; it is as brown as a berry, as is the more russet *I.* 'Autumn Leaves'.

LEFT: *Bursting from their prickly skins, the ripe seeds of the sweet chestnut* (Castanea sativa) *are a richly burnished brown.*
OPPOSITE: Iris *'Wild Ginger' has petals of a rare velvety brown.*

BLACK

Black is the color of mourning in the puritan West, the color of death and grief, of Sunday best and city suits. It is the color of dangerous magic and ill luck; the color of coal, soot, and charcoal—the raw materials and residues of the flare of fire. It is also the conventional color of decadence, of sexy underwear, of bad guys in films, the uniform of undertakers and priests, and chic and slinky style— whoever saw a farmer or a gardener go to work in black?

It is everything that cannot be seen. Black pigment totally absorbs light, making every black a fathomless hole of light. It is a presence as much as a color and yet we know exactly what we mean by black in color terms. It is the only measurable color in the spectrum. There are no shades of black, no subjectivity or interpretation needed, only matt or glossy darkness. The petals of *Viola* 'Penny Black' stand as the mattest black in the garden and have a fabulous intensity. The shiniest are either the polished stems of the bamboo *Phyllostachys nigra*, which grow darker as they mature, or the glistening branches of ash on a wet dusk in early spring, sheathed in shiny black.

With the exception of *Ophiopogon planiscapus* 'Nigrescens', whose spiky, grass-like leaves are genuinely black, there are in fact very few black plants or even any that have bits that are blackish. Like *Phyllostachys nigra*, the dogwood *Cornus*

alba 'Kesselringii' has purple-black stems. The berries of some ivies turn black and those of the holly *Ilex crenata* are always black. The name of *Iris* 'Black Knight' gives a hint as to its color, and *I.* 'Sabre' is a purple deep enough to appear black. I have never seen them, but apparently the catkins of the black willow (*Salix gracilistyla* 'Melanostachys') are black. It is difficult to use these plants as part of a color harmony since they get lost in a summer garden. As novelties in a corner, though, they would be good, sinister fun.

Otherwise it is only when it snows that we get to notice black in the garden. The bare branches of most deciduous trees seem black against a snow-laden sky with the reflection of white from the ground. Water becomes mirrored tar and all shades of brown and gray are flattened to black. It is lovely, a visual representation of the simplification of life's complexities to black and white.

OPPOSITE: *The stark black outline of tree trunks and naked branches against a backdrop of snow is the nearest a garden ever gets to monochrome.*
RIGHT: Helleborus orientalis *(top) varies in color from pale pink to a purple so dark that it appears black. The blue-black petals of the bromeliad* Puya alpestris *(center) are made much richer by the violent contrast to the orange stamens. The leaves of* Ophiopogon planiscarpus nigrescens *(bottom) are a freak show: attractive for their oddity; it's by far the most common black garden plant.*

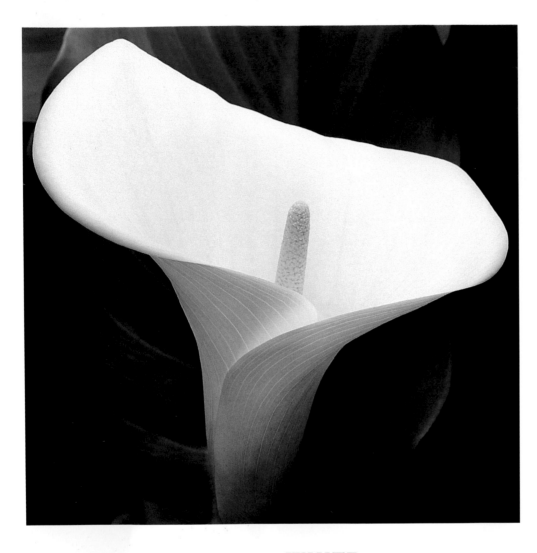

ABOVE: *White is a matter of degrees, perfected only by the absolute absence of other colors. This arum-lily (Zantedeschia aethiopica) is made to appear white by the pale green and cream colors and the rude orange of its spadix.*

WHITE

In Western cultures white brings with it associations of cleanliness, clarity, purity, goodness, and truth—a "white" lie is a forgivable untruth, the good cowboy rides a white horse. Clearly our response to white—or any color—is not best understood in terms of color science. We all think that we know white when we see it. Yet in the garden anything from light gray to quite a yellowy cream passes muster as white. Most white flowers are in fact creamy white, a warm color, slightly yellowish or ivory. White shines much more brightly under gray skies than under fierce light and blue skies; this is why white often is at its best when the sun is low or in shade.

White light is made up of all the colors of the spectrum. Pass white light through a prism and all the constituent colors come tumbling out. Mix all the colors on a palette together and you will certainly not get white—the result will instead be a muddy brown. So we must not confuse the effect of light waves and pigments.

We tend to see white not as a mixture of colors but as the absence of any particular color combined with the presence of light. The quality of this light is what usually defines the white to our eye, rather than the quality of color—which is strongly influenced by neighboring colors. The measure of this is seen in snow. We use the term "snow-white" to mean absolutely unblemished white, but in fact snow is usually strongly tinged with blue and often with pink or yellow, according to the quality of the light. Snow is a symbol of purity rather than a description of a pure color. Yet for most gardeners, the first hour of snowfall or the dawning of a hoar frost is the nearest they will get to an absolute white. It is without reference, unknowable, yet intensely experienced.

There are more varieties of plants especially bred white than there are for any other color, satisfying the demand for gardeners to feel good as much as for their gardens to look good. There are white delphiniums, wonderful white roses like *Rosa* 'Iceberg', *R.* 'Alba Semiplena', and *R.* 'Blanche Double de Coubert'; white chrysanthemums like *C.* 'Pavilion' and white daisies such as *Tanacetum parthenium* 'Rowallane'. You can have white cosmos (*Cosmos bipinnatus* 'White Sensation'), white foxgloves, and white lupines such as *Lupinus* 'Noble Maiden'. If a plant can be induced to produce white flowers, no effort is spared in making it do so, in the sure knowledge that the gardening public will buy it voraciously. White combines perfectly with green and is at its best in the shade. It is hardly surprising that it is the most popular of all plant colors.

If you are planning an area of pure white, you could do worse than to look at a piece of undisturbed ground in May. The first thing you will notice is that despite the abundance of white, there is considerably more green. The truth is that a "white" garden is really a "green with a lot of white and no other colors to distract" garden. In painterly terms, you can add an enormous amount of white to green without reducing its essential greenness. So to make the white seem even whiter, the trick is to use all the glaucous (gray) greens and pale greens.

In turn, white colors retain their truest appearance against green. With various shades of green this picks up the subtleties of the tones, giving depth to what might otherwise become a monochromatic picture.

Although you can use white flowers to soften neighboring colors and make them paler, do not fall into the trap of thinking that white brightens an area of planting. Depending on the proportions, white can strengthen and deepen adjacent colors and this may have the effect of actually making them seem darker.

LEFT: *Snowdrops* (Galanthus nivalis) *in snow have an icy delicacy, yet despite their seeming fragility, they are exceptionally tough plants.*
ABOVE: Rosa rugosa *'Alba' shares the snowdrop's robustness yet is as exquisite a flower as any in the garden.*

PINK

Feminine, soft, and delicate: the conventions of pink have no hard edges to them. But why have we appropriated these fluffy images for pink? Does it merit it? After all, its parentage is red and white, colors of heat and aggression and purity respectively: we would hardly expect their offspring to be so pretty.

Red has a vast capacity to absorb white, and pinkness has an enormous range. Because we acknowledge pink as a separate color, there are a whole class of pale reds that we identify mainly by recognizing that they are not pink, and every shade of red

when it is combined with white will produce a different pink, with red itself veering from orange to magenta, and carrying a thousand pinks with it.

Pink is passive. Visually it hardly influences neighboring color at all (although it inevitably creates an influence of tone or mood), and yet it absorbs influence dramatically. It is made darker by whites and silver, redder by plenty of green around it, and brighter by gray. When a touch of yellow is added to pink it becomes warmer and silvery—the color of so many wonderful pink roses like 'Souvenir de la Malmaison' and 'New Dawn'.

Pink with blue in it is cooler and more austere. These are the pinks that mingle so often with violets, lilacs, lavenders—the pastel gamut. They are also the shocking pinks, strutting into magenta, but more of that anon.

Whatever the shade, most people need pink in the garden to soften the edges, to induce relaxation. This is because its message is immediate and undemanding. It asks very little of the eye and less of the mind, save admiration. Think of a garden devoid of pink. It would certainly have vigor and even some subtlety and depth, but it would be devoid of a crucial range of sensuousness.

Pink coaxes hedonism out of even the most gruff. I know of little that has such uncomplicated beauty as a mixed bowl of old pink roses: albas, gallicas, bourbons, centifolias, and damasks. It is the nearest the gardener ever comes to visual bliss.

These lupines create a powerful flutter of pink, yet a second look shows that they scan the palette from yellow to purple, proving that pink is a sensation as much as a color analysis.

RED

Red is the color of anger and warning, of change and revolution, the color of fire and blood. It is the most forward of colors in the garden, spreading out from a single flower like huge ripples from a little stone. Yet it is invisible to bees, which perceive it as black.

The vegetable garden is red in tooth and claw. Tomatoes, red peppers, radishes, beets, plums, and cherries span from vermilion through to ruby. It is worth planting ruby chard for entertainment value alone. Its purple-veined green leaves fan the astonishing brilliance of the stems and will last for months, regrowing

Red foliage is hard to come by except in autumn, although most vines can be relied upon to blaze bright red for a week or more. One of the best reds comes after many of the leaves have fallen: on the stems of dogwood (*Cornus alba* 'Sibirica'), which seem all the more vivid against a harsh frosty backdrop.

So red must be used in the garden with passion and complete shamelessness. It is hard to do otherwise, for red always leaps forward (especially, by the way, to people who are short-sighted) and can therefore be tricky if it has more retiring colors around it. It has to be used judiciously. In practice this means not mixing it in a spotty way with pastel colors, but allying strength with strength. Best of all is red against a green background: you only have to look at holly berries against their shiny green leaves to understand this.

when cut back. The flowers of runner beans justify their cultivation, too, and strawberries, redcurrants, and raspberries are as decorative as they are delicious.

Radicchio is easy to grow and provides late-summer ruddiness. I grow 'Worcester Pearmain' apples both to eat off the tree in late summer and to be able to marvel at their red voluptuousness.

Annuals produce the brightest range of reds because they have most need to hustle for germination in their few months of flowering. This makes a fierce, almost pure display that can be lovely.

OPPOSITE: *Looking as lividly unreal as a computer-generated hologram, these dying leaves of* Acer palmatum *are a defiant shout of color.*
ABOVE: *However strong, no color exists in isolation in the garden. The tiniest variation in hue will affect our perception of the entire image. The curiously flattened berries of* Gaultheria mucronata *'Bells Seedling' (left) have their redness defined by the blue/green of the leaves and the very yellow stalks. The red stems of ruby chard (center) are almost fluorescent against their young purple leaves. Translucent redcurrants in a grid of pale green baskets (right) are overlaid by a delicate tracery of stalks, resembling an infrared satellite picture.*

ORANGE

Orange is, of course, a mixture of red and yellow, but as it darkens it tends toward brown rather than red, becoming almost sienna. The wonderful sunflower *Helianthus* 'Velvet Queen' is a rich, bronzy brown and yet has clearly come via orange. Some of the rudbeckias, such as *R. hirta* 'Marmalade' or the mixed 'Rustic Dwarfs', have this same orangey bronze coloring that is fantastically invigorating.

There is a temptation to get too subtle and sophisticated with bronzes, marmalades, and topazes when orange— plain, brash orange—is vulgar and gutsy and should be enjoyed as such. That is why I love nasturtiums (*Tropaeolum majus*) and the African and French marigolds (*Tagetes erecta* and *patula* respectively). I sow them late in the vegetable garden where they blaze until hammered into submission by a really hard succession of frosts. Any sophistication would dim their light. Yet orange roses are rarely a success, because, I think, they make an unhappy combination of brashness and sophistication. They are fishes out of water, too chalky and refined for the desired gusto that orange relishes. This is the essence of orange and its role in the garden: it has to be wholehearted and natural, or it falls at the first hurdle.

Orange looks good low down in a border, muted by surrounding plants. Sticking out over the top of other plants it will merely look hysterical, but

hunkered down by the ground it shines with pure color rather than light. Zinnias, eschscholzias, violas, calendulas, and nasturtiums all perform well here. One of the best autumnal examples of this is a field of orange pumpkins sitting on the ground like a colony of garish, hugely overgrown chicks.

Orange climbers almost always look odd, like a zany traffic light. It is, again, because they are too exposed to the light, too "up there" to be taken seriously in northern light. It is no coincidence that most truly orange-flowered climbers are escapees from the tropics.

In the full glare of the bright summer sun, orange is best dotted in among the restrained blues, grays, and yellows, where it will invigorate rather than clash. *Geum* 'Borisii', seemingly suspended and floating above its foliage rather than on the end of its long stems, is wonderfully effective in this role. *Rudbeckia hirta* is less ethereal (if orange could ever be described as such), but equally effective with its almost bronze hue.

OPPOSITE: *The petals of a dahlia tread an orange spiral as controlled as a dance, the shadows and highlights counted out in pure color.*
LEFT: *Redness in autumn leaves is caused by an accumulation of sugars, which decomposing chlorophyll fails to mask. The greater the difference between day and nighttime temperatures the greater the intensity of autumn color.*

YELLOW

Compared with humans, most mammals are bad at differentiating color, although a surprisingly high percentage of men are color blind. But very few people, male or female, have trouble identifying yellow. We know that we do not "see" with the eye, that it is merely a tool for collecting visual information and that it is the brain that organizes and uses that information to give it meaning. Therefore, there must be some psychological reason why yellow matters to us. The eye sees it and we gobble it up greedily. Of all the colors, yellow is the one that presents least problems in differentiating among its various hues. Yellow should be splashed about. Our response to it is uncomplicated and immediate. Too little is niggardly and too much is sinister.

We associate yellow primarily with spring, and consequently with newness, vibrancy, and hope. It is, in fact, the brightest color, advertising energy, and extraversion. Chrome yellow is technically the most visible color on earth. It is the color of the sun and just when we have least sun in the sky I love the way that little stars of yellow start popping up out of the ground. Aconites, crocuses, daffodils, primroses, yellow tulips, trollius, winter jasmine, forsythia, stachyurus, mahonia, buttercups, yellow flags (*Iris pseudocorus*), cowslips, dandelions—all are yellow against green foliage or bare branches. There is a purity and strength about this that is utterly heartening, feeding me with the strength to battle on, through to spring proper.

There are negative connotations to yellow as well. It is the color of cowardice and jealousy. A yellow rose is the symbol

of infidelity. It is the color of warning and quarantine: in nature, yellow is a poisonous color and is used to scare off would-be predators. Perhaps this is why yellow is the least popular color for clothing, particularly the darker shades.

Yellow flowers in high summer are rarely successful on their own in the way that they are in spring. The green of leaves becomes too blue and the shadows are too black. Summer yellow is best mingled with purples and blues, reds, oranges, violet, and magenta, but it rarely works with pink.

I love the nostalgic yellowness of early autumn, the xanthophyll in the leaves coming to the fore as the sugars intensify and the chlorophyll dies, leaving the leaves to slide toward autumn proper, arousing gentle sorrow without the taint of grief. Highlights at this time of year include *Clematis* 'Bill Mackenzie', which will keep its lantern-shaped yellow flowers into midwinter in a mild region, and the holly *Ilex aquifolium* 'Bacciflava', which has yellow berries like clusters of tiny lemons, a harbinger of the hidden spring to come.

The great sweep of garden yellows. From left to right we progress through the surprising delicacy of color of the helianthus, via the soft warmth of fallen ginkgo leaves, past the punchy brilliance of a gourd flower and the intensity of the crocus, through to the trollius that sits at the edge of orange until at last you leave yellow behind and arrive at the almost orange of the ornithogalum.

GREEN

The story of the garden is a green one. All other colors are diversions from this main narrative. Good gardeners have fingers or thumbs colored only green.

Green manages to be the color both of calm and of newness. It is the color of nature, of inexperience and youth, and nothing so characterizes the first growing months of the year—April, May, June—as their overwhelming greenness.

Every other color and color combination is set against this backdrop. It is an assumption. No allowances are necessary. But if that greenness were not there, how we should notice its absence!

A whole division of plant types is given to evergreens, those plants that retain their leaves throughout winter. Most evergreens do in fact shed their leaves annually, but only after or as the new ones appear, so that the transfer appears seamless. With the plentiful and judicious use of evergreens such as box, yew, holly, ivy, or Portuguese laurel (*Prunus lusitanica*) you can give the garden a consistency of color as well as some structure. Infill these with grass and you have the essence of a garden with all other colored plants merely periodical decorations.

In high summer this is an absurd reduction of sensuous opportunity, but in winter it is a stark necessity. A garden with a strong architecture of midwinter green has a balance that gets lost in the clutter of summer color.

Greenhouses are now places of light and a steely brightness but originated in the seventeenth century to house "greens"—chiefly citruses—and protect them from the northern cold. They were built of brick with windows only in their south side. In time they became heated and were given more light.

Green can be used as a positive force rather than just infill between "proper" colors. Take grass. Other than as a playground I have always considered lawns to be most important within the scheme of a garden as a visual calmative. No other color is as restful to the eye. No other color has so many identifiable shades or tones on display, ranging from almost blue to almost yellow. This color range is increased by the effect of light and shade,

adding to the astonishing variety. It soothes and placates without ever being dull (in the way that, surprisingly, jangled colors can be). Green creates the balance and tonal space between colors that is essential, and in a large garden you need the openness of a lawn to slow things down; otherwise you dissolve into a whirl of frantic horticultural business.

Because most leaves are green, we are nearly always surprised to find green flowers, although there are a number of plants that are anarchic green in flower, many of them with viridiflora somewhere about their names. There are the hellebores *H. corsicus, H. foetidus,* and *H. viridis,* of which the last is the most unequivocally green. A few clematis have green flowers, notably *C. cirrhosa* in winter and *C. florida* 'Alba Plena' in summer. *Moluccella laevis* or 'Bells of Ireland' is an annual that is easy to grow from seed and seems to have vivid green flowers, although in fact the green is from the calyx surrounding tiny white flowers. An annual with true green leaves is the zinnia 'Envy'. The Viridiflora tulips have some green in them, of which 'Spring Green' (white, feathered green) appears the greenest. Three fritillaries are really green—*F. cirrhosa, F. pallidiflora,* and *F. pontica.* A summer corm growing green is *Gladiolus* 'Green Isle', and *Galtonia viridiflora* is a summer-flowering bulb with pale green bells for flowers. More pale green flowers are found on *Nicotiana langsdorffii* and among the 'Sensation' series of tobacco plants is 'Lime Green' which, unsurprisingly, also has true green flowers.

OPPOSITE: *Although ubiquitous in the garden, green is rarely the final color for a fruit or flower. Gooseberries (top) break that rule as do the flowerheads of Zinnia elegans 'Envy' (bottom).*
LEFT: *Representing both ends of green's broad spectrum, golden hop lies across the glaucous leaves of* Hosta sieboldiana *(top). The overall greenness of the beautiful* Euphorbia characias wulfenii *(bottom) is accentuated by the tiny red-brown nectar glands.*

BLUE

Absolute blue has to be hunted down and used as a floral jewel amid a range spanning from the blue-green of *Hosta sieboldiana* leaves to the blue-purple of so many plants. Blue is conventionally a cool, distancing color, but as red is added to the pigment, it warms up considerably until you reach purple, which is overtly rich and hot. If you add yellow instead, blue becomes less intense and dislocated until you reach the utter harmony of green. Clearly, there comes a point when the eye differentiates and labels a color lavender, mauve, lilac, or purple rather than blue, but it is an imprecise and subjective thing.

Unarguably pure blue, or ultramarine (the blue of lapis lazuli, more precious than gold and a blue so rare that in medieval paintings it was reserved exclusively for the Virgin's mantle), is almost imperial in assurance and authority. But as soon as blue becomes less than pure it assumes a vagueness, almost a diffidence. Blue resists definition, avoids description: the Greeks had no word for it; and in all the hundreds of references to the sky in the Bible never once is blue mentioned. Birds cannot see true blue—only an oily yellow substitute. Bees see only in blue and yellow. Blue evades us, is out of reach, is nowhere.

So what does this do to us? Why is blue the one color with which we can label a feeling? We know exactly what

having "the blues" means, yet at the same time we can be elevated by the beauty of blue. But it will be through admiration rather than intimacy.

Blue draws the eye out, away from other colors, so that too much blue can have rather a fretful effect. On a large scale, in sea or sky, this is restful and inspiring, but in the claustrophobic space of a garden it can be uncomfortable. A blue border would become like a table set with blue food—indigestible and disturbing. But it is almost impossible to have an area dominated by blue, even with a mass of bluebells, cornflowers, meconopsis, or delphiniums. There is too much green to hand for that and the sky is too often a shade of gray not to have a powerful leavening effect.

True blue flowers are few and far between. There is a reward of a million dollars for the first blue tulip and there is no true blue rose or carnation. "Blue" hostas in any other context would be green. The Himalayan poppy (*Meconopsis betonicifolia*) is always cited as the plant with the "purest" blue, but perhaps the flower with the most blue pigment to be saturated with light is *Anchusa azurea* 'Loddon Royalist'. It needs a well-drained, not-too-rich soil for optimum color.

Meconopsis grandis is an unequivocal blue. Its hue is icily pure and a yardstick by which to measure how seldom blue is found in nature.

PURPLE

My parents' garden was dominated by a huge purple beech. The purple mound of leaves was a mark of domesticity in a countryside of green beech wood. Aerial photographs show purple trees as marks of suburbanization as vividly as the flat blue of swimming pools.

We know what we think purple is, but we struggle to define its boundaries—to know what it isn't. One man's purple is another man's violet—or mauve. Royal purple—color of majesty in ancient Rome—was probably not purple as we describe it, but more akin to blue. Collected from the shellfish murex and boiled for dye, it was fabulously precious.

Purple is a split personality, half fiery red and half icy blue, neither one nor the other. Purple and red go strongly together—witness the red borders at Hidcote, which are as much purple as red—but purple makes blue less blue. The result can be intense, but lacks blue's purity. Violet is purple edging to blue and mauve is purple overloaded with red. Mix them all together in a border and you have a shimmering, shot-silk mixture.

The truth is that one rarely uses purple on its own. It is nearly always there to allow other colors to show through more powerfully. Even the great purple plants—iris, buddleia, *Clematis jackmanii*, lavender—are all offset by their green foliage, which is usually a glaucous tone. Purple and its variations are the colors of shade—their presence casts shade and they should be used accordingly. Shade need not be synonymous with gloom, but will never leap out at you. It is the color of depth and recesses and if used well adds intensity to colors set before it.

Purple is the darkest color in the spectrum, but bright sunlight dulls it and is wasted on it. It needs the long shadows of evening or the weak sun of early autumn to show it off to best effect.

Gertrude Jekyll disapproved of purple as a dominant color, to the loss of any garden she designed. Think of purple tulips, wallflowers, bearded irises, asters, salvias, alliums, dahlias, clematis, cotinus, delphiniums, purple loosestrife, purple basil, lavatera—what a waste not to use their deep intensity throughout the year, mingled with reds and orange.

OPPOSITE: *No plant wears purple with such imperial grandeur as* Iris reticulata. *Each tongue is marked like a flight path for pollinators to land on.* RIGHT: *The flowers of* Clematis integrifolia *(top left) fall toward the blue end of the purple scale, with only a touch of red that defines it as mauve rather than blue. The emerging petals of this iris (top right) are an intense violet, where red slightly dominates the purple more than blue. The orange centers of the flowers of the Chilean potato tree (*Solanum crispum*) (bottom) accentuate the blue within the purple, creating an overall image that is predominantly mauve.*

Magenta is a weapon, a potentially dangerous instrument of color. In the wrong hands it can destroy.

MAGENTA

It is remarkable how much animosity a color can arouse. Gertrude Jekyll hated magenta too, calling it "malignant." Many other, lesser gardeners affect to disdain it. It is hard to see why this should be. Magenta is what happens to pink when it absorbs as much blue as it can without becoming violet or purple. Where pink is restful and soft, magenta is a shock wave in the border. Often bundled carelessly in with pink, it stands alone as perhaps the most difficult color in the gardener's spectrum and consequently, rather than deserving opprobrium, it is one of the most interesting. But why isolate it as worthy of special treatment? Why not include it as an extreme version of pink? Partly because there is such a strong body of plants that cannot be described as any other color and also because it pulls a particular trigger on the senses that needs understanding if it is to be used to maximum effect.

However you use magenta (and there are no rights or wrongs—only your sensations) it is a weapon, a potentially dangerous instrument of color. In the wrong hands it can destroy. Used with skill it adds life and vibrancy where pink can suffocate with softness and red can be altogether too jolly.

Lychnis coronaria is the epitome of magenta, with *Geranium psilostemon*, *G. macrorrhizum*, *Nicotiana alata*, *Cosmos* 'Sensation', lupines, *Rosa rugosa*, *R.* 'Gypsy Boy', *R.* 'Rose de Rescht', and *Rhododendron* 'Roseum Elegans' all defining the color.

Magenta is one of the richest of colors; it is garish and a little of it goes a long way. Too much is as indigestible as a surfeit of chocolate pudding. It has the ability to change color in response to light, almost like litmus paper, so that in the sun its redness comes forward and as it falls into shade the blueness slides out, making it violet. Everything is always complicated. But magenta has a kind of perverse simplicity. It is always unquestionably Not Pink and Not Red.

Perhaps the best way to use it is to dot it in a border, mixing it with lemons and oranges and purples, adding a thrill of drama to what might otherwise be a too-safe color scheme.

LEFT TO RIGHT: *Magenta is a carnival of a color, partying until it drops. Cistus, the marvelously sculptural lupines, and an allium each dance out at you. The secret is to go with its outrageous spirit and splash it across the garden.*

COMBINATIONS

You can never isolate a single color in the garden. Apart from the combination of different flowers and their foliage there are elements such as the sky, the soil, washing on the line, and the clothes people wear to take into account.

If this were not enough, our own eyes can deceive us. After looking at an intense block of color we see a faint after-image of its complementary—an effect known as successive contrast. Violet brings on a yellow after-image and a ghostly orange follows blue. This may well spoil the carefully constructed effect that you are straining for. So, for example, the complementary color of limey yellow is magenta, which does not work well with a purer pink. Although you may not have a hint of magenta visible, the after-image caused by the yellow will make the pink seem uncomfortable.

The combination of color opposites, however, has a particularly vibrant freshness. One thinks of daffodils growing with scillas, bright yellow tulips with blue hyacinths, or lavender with senecio. Some plants have the two colors built in. Any red flower contrasts vividly with its green leaves, so that the whole plant vibrates with a dynamic harmony. The two colors are very similar tonally (try establishing the difference in a black and white photograph), so it is the color alone that carries the weight of their contrast. Think of scarlet tulips, *Salvia fulgens,* and blood-red poppies in this context, as well as holly berries.

Yellow and red is a less common mixture, making traditionally "hot" colors, although it is the orange that is hot, not the separate components. The first sighting of them together is usually with tulips and wallflowers (although the latter are more often orange than red). In spring this is garish, vulgar, and lovely. The same combination by midsummer becomes rich and musky. The vermilion dahlia 'Bishop of Llandaff' with its licorice stems and leaves, orange day lilies (*Hemerocallis*), and scarlet crocosmias like *C.* 'Lucifer' all typify this hot high-summer color.

Gertrude Jekyll prepared the eye for an area of gray with pools of yellow and orange plants. The glaucous foliage is made purer by the afterglow in the mind of the yellow you have just seen.

One afterglow the eye should never have to recall is the one left by the combination of yellow and bright pink. Where you have two strong colors in a border, a block of white will separate them cleanly so that their contrast does not injure them. White dotted in among another color will dilute it and change it. The obvious example is to mix white and red to make pink.

Mixing blue and white has the effect of making the white seem whiter. All the purveyors of laundry soap cottoned onto this and have long been selling us the concept of "blue whiteness," even though this is clearly nonsense. Thankfully, the antiseptic wholesomeness of the combination is invariably leavened by a strong dose of green foliage. But every gardener since Vita Sackville-West has learned to make their white garden wash whiter with the judicious use of blue. It is much less common to find a garden that is deliberately planted as blue and white, but the overall effect is gentle and tranquil.

Despite the "blue and green should never be seen" rule, they invariably are mixed, with no noticeable collapse of moral order. Just the two colors together make a soft but inconclusive jangle. But put orange into the mix and things at once pull together.

Orange and pink make uncomfortable flower-bedfellows. Orange makes pink saccharine and coy, and pink brings the slut out of orange. Nevertheless, both do very well with deep crimsons and purples. The greens of late summer—when most purple is about—are not up to the inspiration it needs, whereas the same colors in late spring or early summer would glow. However, put just one orange marigold in the purple mix and the whole thing takes off.

OPPOSITE: *Reds taken through the gamut from purple to pink combine to provide almost a surfeit of riches.*

BELOW: *Conversely, colors that might be considered brighter, actually make a cooler combination.*

PASTELS

The very word is gentle. No army ever went to war dressed in a fetching combination of pastel shades. Pinks, soft yellows, lilac, lavender, and powdery blues all fit the bill. All are pale, chalky colors and have a fuzziness of texture; no pastel color could be glossy. By definition they are all muted in hue and they beckon the eye to them rather than leaping out and mugging you with color. On the other hand, pastels need not be delicate or subtle. Indeed, at times there can be an almost aggressive pastelness caused by the contrast between the hard, green foliage and the pastel of the flowers, as in many rhododendrons, or the pink pompoms of *Bellis perennis*.

But for many people floral softness is the essence of beauty. It makes a visual retreat from the abrasive edge of the world and defines their peace. For most of us, though, this is just part of the color balance of the garden. If we use the full range of visual sensation, we must have some combinations of color that are soft and balanced in tone and hue. Too many are like a surfeit of marshmallows, too little and we have wasted some of the garden's potential.

Pastels can easily look washed out and thin in the harsh midday sun. This is why they favor the gardens of the northern hemisphere, where light never burns with the intensity of the tropics. Even in the north, they look at their best when the sun is low, either in the morning or evening. On the whole, morning sunlight does pastel colors the most justice, lending them delicacy and shadow. In the evening the darker colors disappear, while the whites increase in luminosity and the balance and interplay of color is lost. So, if you live in the northern hemisphere, plant pastels facing east.

White can be used almost without limit with pastel shades. It is a component of each pastel color and can be added indefinitely without the color balance ever becoming overwhelmingly white.

Foliage is a vital part of the pastel mix. Rather than acting as a contrast or divider for the colors, it is best used as a component of the tonal combination. Glaucous greens, silver, and variegated leaves work best. Plants like artemisia, the curry plant (*Helichrysum italica*), the trailing *H. petiolare*, santolina, lychnis, or the lovely giant thistles (*Onopordum*) all earn their keep here for their foliage alone, interspersed with pastel flowers.

TOP LEFT: *Soft light brings out the delicacy in these campanulas. The overall effect is rich but the individual petals are delicately tinted.*
BOTTOM LEFT: *Almost all pastel combinations work together, making it possible to let plants mingle indiscriminately. Here achillea and oenothera artlessly combine.*
OPPOSITE: *For many people the softness of pastel shades is the prime factor of beauty in the garden.*

JEWEL COLORS

Rich greens, oranges, purples, velvety crimsons, and the occasional intense blue are all jewel colors—emerald, topaz, amethyst, ruby, and sapphire—throwing out strong color but little light. True blue, being such a rare color to find in gardens, only just makes it into this grouping but meconopsis shining out of a shady border or *Anchusa azurea* 'Loddon Royalist' dazzling the eye with the intensity of its blueness will make a little go a long way.

I spent ten years as a jewelry designer and grew to love the rich clash of these colors, which individually are formal almost to the point of somberness but powerfully bright when they are put together.

It is rare to find a border that is planted with just these colors. But it can be done and to great effect. The trick is to eliminate anything that does not fit the jewel-like prescription, which means omitting all whites, pinks, yellows, and pastel shades of any hue. That wipes out three quarters of the world's plant inventory, but from what remains the choice is wide enough.

Certain flower species major in these colors and a jewel garden can be created from a very limited range of plants. I am thinking of violas, salvias, primulas, clematis, cornflowers, wallflowers, antirrhinums, dahlias, tulips, and irises. As ever, blue is in short supply in this list, but it can be injected into the mix with selected plants such as *Salvia patens*, *Viola* 'Azure Blue', and the low-growing petunia 'Blue Daddy'.

The second secret is to position plants with jewel colors where they will get evening light. You want to achieve intensity of experience rather than garishness, subtlety, or plain brightness and that intensity can only be fully savored in the slanting shadows of evening.

You do not have to mingle all the colors in one go. There are pairs and single combinations that will provide the richness you are after. The perfect example of this is English holly (*Ilex aquifolium*), whose shiny green leaves and bright red berries so powerfully symbolize life in the dead core of winter. The berries of hawthorn, pyracantha, and cotoneaster, the hips of roses and edible fruits such as raspberry and redcurrants all work powerfully for the same reason—the contrast between red and green. Most plants with red flowers or fruit have green leaves

which make the red seem redder. If these plants are placed against a more general green background they stand out all the more, and the vermilion flowers of geum, poppy, or Jerusalem cross (*Lychnis chalcedonica*) blaze out from the collective green of the general border foliage.

There are certain tricks that the National Trust gardeners have employed in the famous red borders at Hidcote Manor in Gloucestershire that are worth learning. The first is that red containing yellow should never be mixed with red containing blue. Therefore the vermilion of *Lychnis chalcedonica* (red containing yellow) cannot rub shoulders with *Lobelia* 'Cherry Ripe' (red containing blue). I am inherently suspicious of hard and fast rules and enjoy seeing them broken, but it is certainly worth experimenting with this maxim as a guide, if not as a binding piece of legislation.

Purple leaves used with conviction and as a foil to other colors can add real depth to a garden. Purple beech makes a much better hedge than it does a tree if it is clipped tight and used as backdrop to reds and oranges. It is not a restful, easy color like green, and it tends to absorb light, so the colors used against it must be strong enough to pull forward from it. With the jewel colors purple adds subtlety and depth where green merely provides contrast.

OPPOSITE LEFT: *The berries of* Mahonia x media *'Charity' are an extraordinarily intense powder blue—almost exactly the color-opposite of the flowers that made them.*
OPPOSITE RIGHT: *The intense red dots of pheasant's eye (*Adonis annua*) float above its feathered green foliage.*
RIGHT: *A perfect example of the jewel-like setting of wildflowers in a meadow. Poppies, cornflowers, and daisies flourish in poor quality, well-drained soil.*

The intensity of jewel colors can be savored only in the slanting shadows of evening.

COLOR RIOTS

The jangling clash of colors that self-consciously tasteful gardeners have tried to eliminate for years is now—thank heavens—coming back into favor. We are all too solemn about gardening, acting as though diligence and erudition are more important than having fun. So many "great" gardens are boring simply because they omit this vital element.

The senses need gaudy joy as much as they need calm and ease. By juxtaposing oranges, purples, brilliant blues, magentas, scarlets, and shocking pinks you grab color by the scruff of the neck and shake it. This injects excitement and danger, adding that essential sense of adventure to the gardening process.

There are two times of year when this is most effective, spring and early autumn. The spring timing is almost entirely due to the presence of electric lime-green foliage that is charged with yellow. By summer this has matured into a grown-up green, with all the zaniness of youth put away. It makes the most exciting foil for the splashes of color from spring bulbs, early annuals, and the more brilliant perennials that are emerging. In early autumn the garden has a second childhood and many of the best oranges and bright yellows come into their own, including sunflowers, red hot pokers, rudbeckias, ligularias, and dahlias. Hollyhocks hang as gaudy towers of color into bare-branched autumn. And with the intensity and garishness of some of the asters and gladioli, petunias, purple *Verbena bonariensis*, and the late flowers of *Rosa* 'Souvenir du Docteur Jamain' added to the oranges, magentas, and glaring vermillions of berries, and the extraordinary vividness of the turning leaves, especially maples, you can challenge the notion that autumn is a gentle slide into winter.

In spring, bright green, pink, scarlet, and a touch of orange are as invigorating as cold water splashed in the face. Red and orange tulips are a cosmic joke, goblets of fire balanced on impossibly thin stems. Lime-green *Euphorbia polychroma* and orange-tipped *E. griffithii* 'Fireglow' seem to be brushes charged to paint dazzling graffiti; nothing is serious, everything aflame with sensation. If the colors are arresting enough—like autumnal oranges, burnt yellows, and purple—green is a backdrop to the rest of the picture, while in spring it is a riotous color in its own right.

Blue is hard to work into a color riot, partly because there is not enough of it to go around in the carefree way that these combinations require. At the time when orange is most available—late summer and autumn—there is more purple and violet available than blue. In spring wallflowers clash cheerfully with the available blue, and there are orange tulips, orange pansies, and the marvelous *Geum* 'Borisii' to use as well.

Kitchen gardens often provide more midsummer jollity than a lot of borders. Scarlet-flowered beans in wigwams of brilliant color, sweet peas, ruby chard, tomatoes, beets, and pumpkins make an anarchy of color, unmannered, often unplanned, and always the better for it.

OPPOSITE: *Orange dahlias and magenta cosmos make the perfect late summer combination, leavened by their green foliage.*
ABOVE: *Scarlet salvias and orange marigolds are merely hot, but add the purple of* Verbena bonariensis *and the combination becomes bright.*
RIGHT: *Some flowers are intrinsically gaudy on their own, such as Dahlia 'Bishop of Llandaff'.*

STRUCTURE

There is a tendency to associate color in the garden only with flowers. As we have seen, this overlooks the enormous influence of green and brown which between them make up the vast majority of colored area in the garden. It is also to ignore the effect of all the non-flowering objects and components of any garden, in terms not only of color but also of shape and form.

The best advice I ever received about gardening was to plant the "bones" early and not to worry about the details; they could adapt and change as inclination, time, and experience allowed. But by creating a strong structure of hedges, walls, and fences, linked by paths, you set the scene. As I become more and more experienced, I realize that we often over-elaborate. The structure alone can be enough. A garden is a place, not a collection of plants, and the creation of place can be as simple or complex as you want it to be. On a practical level, a series of hedges linked by grass that only has to be mown once a week is easily manageable, can be extremely beautiful,

LEFT: *Monumental sculptural shapes carved out of growing plants. A massive yew nipple (top) is as solid as moss-covered stone. Frost-dusted box is clipped into tightly scrolled designs in a parterre (center), and rounded finials balance on massive walls of yew (bottom).*

and has great potential to be developed into areas of complex planting—just by digging through the turf.

It is vital to see the garden as a brand of performance art. It is a series of stage sets upon which there are many different works going on at any one time. If these stages ran unbounded into each other, the whole thing would be a confusing jumble. Hedges, fences, lawns, paths, steps, terraces can help us to get the most from each show.

Although hedges have a color, often green, their visual significance is as much to direct the eye as to entertain it. A hedge or fence will automatically point the eye to where it is not, to a gap or to the conclusion of this visual barrier. By managing this effect we can intensify the performance of a color when the eye finally arrives there.

The shape of each barrier will also have a profound visual effect and it is wrong to plump for the obvious without considering the alternatives. So a hedge might best be square topped—as most garden hedges are—but it could work better to the eye if rounded or cut on a

RIGHT: *From a carefully contrived set of huge chessmen (top), via a meticulously trimmed, almost two-dimensional parterre (center) to the brilliantly effective simplicity of assorted balls (bottom), the structural abstraction of clipped box stresses the vital role of monochromatic structure in a garden.*

batter, castellated, scalloped, or with windows cut in it. It might be planted in a straight line but could just as easily be crinkle-crankle. You have to consider whether to impose hedges on the landscape—such as yew or box—or to select hedging material that blends into the plant life in the locality, which is likely to be more mixed and informal. Indeed, the locality might be an urban jungle or a plot by the edge of the ocean: whatever, it must be considered as part of the visual effect of your garden. Every option is worth considering and will have a distinct visual impact on everything around it.

Fences can be made of timber or iron, walls of stone or brick, and can be rendered and painted or left natural. Every choice will change the way the entire garden looks and this consideration is just as important as the effectiveness of the material chosen as a barrier and boundary. Many otherwise beautiful gardens are ruined by an unfortunate choice of fencing.

Choose your materials carefully to complement your house and the other structures in your garden. It is not simply a question of cost—even the most expensive fencing can look out of place and distract attention from the garden.

Paths can be of grass, concrete, gravel, crushed bark, or be cobbled. They can be constructed of warm, orangey pink brick, which can itself look quite different depending on whether it is laid flat or on edge, in herringbone or basketweave fashion, or in courses. You might choose stone flagstones, concrete slabs, or irregular "crazy paving." Each of these options used to create a path in exactly the same place will look completely different and—more significantly—will make the entire garden look different. Thus the structure of the garden deserves at least as much visual consideration as the planting. We have a tendency to elevate function above form, which can ruin the best planting scheme. I recall my first visit to a National Trust garden famous

You will want somewhere to sit in the garden. Seats have two visual functions. The first is to be looked at, the second to be looked from. We look at seats much more than we sit on them, although the importance of the latter is stressed rather than what the seat looks like. If a seat looks good you will be drawn to it; it becomes an invitation to stop and view your surroundings. Seats work extremely well as the focal point of a path or vista; they give you something to reach, and from them, you can look back from where you came.

Most seats are sold as white or natural wood. White is a harsh and unyielding color in anything other than flowers in a garden. It is almost always better to paint a seat a color that will either blend in more or stand out as a deliberate contrast. Green—especially one strongly tinged with blue—always looks good, as does blue strongly tinged with green. Think of the leaves of *Hosta sieboldiana* and you have a color that is strong when standing alone but which blends into the garden, integrating rather than grating.

Water throws back light and some color, but above all it changes. Even the most stagnant ditch will shift its appearance with the changing light and variations in surrounding growth reflected back out of it. I particularly like shaded pools that receive sunlight for only a few hours a day. This provides a dimension of mystery to a small garden, yet the sunlight prevents it from being a dank, dark corner. Most ponds become covered with a layer of green duckweed (*Lemna minor*) for part of the year, and I love the intense, slightly bobbly sheet of green that this creates.

for its collection of old roses. The roses were certainly magnificent, but they were planted on either side of a wide path made from cinders; it was a dead gray color and annoying to walk on. My overwhelming sensation was of sensuous discomfort and dismay—despite the wonderful flowers.

There are two good exercises that will improve your awareness of the structure of the garden and help you make the most of its contribution. The first is regularly to photograph your garden in black and white. This not only gets rid of the influence of color, forcing you to focus on shapes and textures, but also stresses the importance of tonal qualities between various colors. The second is rigorously to evaluate the garden in midwinter. Instead of this being a period of aesthetic dormancy, there should be enough structure and form to delight you in the complete absence of floral color. I have already referred to the dramatic success of this in the white garden at Sissinghurst.

LEFT TO RIGHT: *Every plant has its own microstructure as well as playing a role in the overall shape of the garden, and all plants deserve to be examined at close range. Here a poppy sheds its protective carapace and unfolds—a wonder of form as much as of color.*

ABOVE: *Snow simplifies everything in the garden down to its bare bones, creating gaunt sculptural forms of fragile temporality. The upright bars of a stick fence are repeated by the icicles from the eaves of a roof that in turn mirror the crisp blank shapes made by the snow in the spaces in the fence.*
OPPOSITE: *For a brief moment of autumnal sunlight shape, light, shadow, and color combine to make a vivid structural image as the reaching branches of a maple hang over the arch of a bridge painted the color of the falling leaves.*

The smallest garden should have some pots in it and a larger one can easily house dozens. The choice of pot is almost as important as the plant it houses. Terracotta never looks bad and is a particularly good foil for green leaves and clear colors. Some pinks can sit uncomfortably with it, though. Plastic pots are for convenience and transportation, not for display. Visually they are thin and insubstantial. But almost anything that will retain soil and allow water to drain can be used to create a visual sensation. Galvanized steel buckets with holes punched in the base, glazed pots, lead urns, barrels, sinks, hollowed tree stumps, an old pair of boots, crates, even a stout cardboard box will all serve their turn as containers. The important thing is to work out what will look best and use it, regardless of preconceived ideas of what ought to be used.

Finally, we do not play nearly enough with our gardens. There are a hundred visual games to be played without using plants (and another hundred with them). You do not need to be a sculptor or to buy sculpture to place artefacts and constructs in among the plants and at strategic points in the garden. Rusty metal always looks very good with green foliage, so keep all broken or ancient tools, let them rust and make mobiles and assemblies in the borders. There is no need to be precious about this—change it every week if you are not satisfied with

it, just as you would train or move plants. Collect driftwood and stones and use them as part of the composition. Any garden ought to be a source of constant visual stimulation. It really does not matter what you use to achieve this: there are no rules.

We are inclined to see what we want to see. Familiarity breeds a kind of blindness as the brain draws on memory rather than perception. Clearly this can be used creatively to fashion an environment that we know will please us. We can fine-tune our visual responses to the point at which they seem to work best and then sit back and let our eyes enjoy rather than inquire.

But this approach can also encourage a reduction of experience, a drawing in of the parameters of experience, so that we literally start to see less and less. Fortunately no garden is ever static for even one day. We might visit other gardens to view them as stage sets that inspire us and then go home and see our own gardens in a new light. But the greatest pleasure in looking at your own garden is observing how it changes. If you have been away for a week the first inclination is to rush outside and see what has come into flower and what has gone, and to luxuriate in the newness of the vision. Ultimately this is the greatest visual gift that a garden has to offer: the invigoration of eye and brain through its power to recreate itself.

SOUND

We tend to think of silence as

being synonymous with peace,

but every gardener knows that no

garden is ever truly silent.

ABOVE: *During summer months every garden is frantic with the busyness of insects gathering*

pollen, accompanied by a medley of hums, drones, buzzes, and high-pitched sawing.

ABOVE: *The stalks of Chinese lanterns (top) will be strummed by the wind. Water is the most controllable element of the garden's music and the plop and flip of fishes rising to the surface (below) is all part of that orchestration.*

OPPOSITE: *There is always some sound in the garden, however small, such as a leaf gently drifting onto still water.*

THE PEACE THAT WE WANT FROM A GARDEN *is the exclusion of unwanted noise, in exactly the same way that we want the exclusion of unwanted people. To enjoy the sounds we want to hear is a form of privacy. We all have our own definition of what is a desirable sound, and generally we will all agree that this is likely to be gentle and musical, but it may be mechanical—after all, the buzz of a far-off mower can be pleasing. I even like to hear the chainsaws in a distant wood, because although a chainsaw can be about the most intrusive and aggressive sound there is, in this context it means that shrubs are being cut back and I associate this activity with a harmony between management and nature. So our own personal associations of sounds will strongly influence our response to them.*

Human hearing is amazingly acute. There is a billionfold alteration from the loudest detectable sound to the faintest, although we have the most limited range of all mammals. Our hearing has in fact evolved to hear best all the possible variations and ranges of speech. Not only can we hear very well, but also the listener can dismiss unwanted sounds to focus on one specific noise. We still hear everything that reaches the ear, but screen the information as it comes in, simultaneously electing how much attention to pay to it. The most obvious example of this is the way, at a party, you can carry on a conversation with a single person, surrounded by a babble of similar isolated conversations, all perfectly audible. Thus, we can listen to wind ruffling through grasses, leaves, a piece of paper jerking across the lawn, and poppy heads swaying gently, and differentiate between each sound, the direction they are coming from, and their relative loudness, while receiving all simultaneously.

This is a miracle of analysis rather than hearing, for it is the brain that organizes and distributes the information and the ear that merely supplies it. From the moment when a sound wave hits the ear to that later moment when the relevant pulse reaches the brain is about one fiftieth of a second. The gap between the two moments is slightly different for each ear, because unless the sound, traveling at 1100 ft. (332 m) per second, is coming from exactly ahead of the listener, it takes fractionally longer to reach the more distant ear. The brain has no problem absorbing and sorting out this information. If you cock your head, the precise location of a sound can be made even more precise, which is why you see a bird listening for worms with its head to one side, or a dog, puzzled by the source of a sound, cock its head to increase the gap between the sound source and its ears.

Although many blind people are supposed to have "better" hearing than sighted people, what in fact happens is that they are forced to use more extensively the audio resources available to us all but which sight renders largely unnecessary. If we listen in the dark or close our eyes outside, the brain takes account of this new, "blind" reality and starts to interpret the audio information with much greater depth and subtlety. Go into the garden and try it. You are bound to discover aspects of the garden that you had overlooked or failed to notice.

WATER

Gardeners sense rain with their ears first. It is the one sound that every gardener curses or rejoices in according to season. Raindrops falling on parched soil at the end of the day is music to the gardener's ears, although the same rain falling just as you are grabbing a precious hour in the garden on ground that has dried sufficiently to work on is a dread sound.

Just as the Inuit have many different words to describe snow, it is an indication of the importance of rain in our society that there are so many words for the action of precipitation: to drizzle, pour, shower, pelt, sheet, bucket, patter, spit, tip, beat, etc. Each description conjures up a different *sound*. Every gardener has lain in bed in the early hours listening to the rain, interpreting the effect on their garden purely by the sound on the roof, windowpanes, or leaves outside. The sound of rain on new leaves in early summer is quite different from the sound of rain on the yellowing, dry leaves of late autumn. In winter the rain slides through the branches to the ground with a muffled patter unknown for half the year. Rain on evergreens, however, is constant, although the brittle slap of raindrops on a shiny leaf like laurel or holly is quite different from the way that yew or box absorbs and muffles the rain, holding the water spongelike and soaking your clothes as you brush against them after the rain has long since stopped.

Raindrops splashing onto puddles pluck wet sounds from wetness. It is an entrancing combination that most gardeners are moved to manufacture at some time. From the very first recorded gardens in Babylon, water has been an essential component of gardens throughout the world. Of course, its reflective stillness is important, too, as are the possibilities it offers for growing aquatic plants, but in every culture you will find the

ABOVE: *A single sheet of water overflowing from a container onto a pool combines a striking image with a pleasing harmony.*
OPPOSITE: *Rain is muffled by the soft foliage of summer before dripping to the ground.*

Raindrops falling on parched soil at the end of the day are music to the gardener's ears.

music of its movement being harnessed. If you are lucky, you will have a natural stream in your garden. This burbles and gurgles as it bounces around rocks and pebbles, and is endlessly calming and fascinating. The sound can be significantly altered by building dams and races; they need not be permanent but create a temporary shift of sound. This allows you the opportunity to indulge in the fun of making them all over again. I spend hours of my grown-up life doing this and do not regret a minute of it.

With the exception of the grandest fountains or cascades like the 276 ft. (84 m) Emperor Fountain at Chatsworth House in Derbyshire, England, moving water nearly always creates an intimate, murmuring sound. It speaks gently to us. This means that it is ideally suited to a smaller garden. A pebble pool, which is a container filled to the brim with pebbles, so that the water splashes over them rather than falling directly into water, can be as small as 12 in. (30 cm) in diameter, with the tank beneath made from a bucket or small trash can. A pump is placed in this, the tank covered with mesh and pebbles laid over it. The water is pumped up into the air and falls back down over the pebbles, filtering back into the tank. Simple, but very effective—and safe for little children.

Even simpler is water flowing from a spout coming out of a wall and falling into a basin. This is very beautiful and

will fit into a tiny back yard. The flow can be adjusted from a slow drip (which could well become maddening) to a splashy gush.

Water can be encouraged to overspill from a succession of ponds and canals in controlled sheets rather than spouts, the sound being accordingly more constant and solid. By varying the size of fall from tank to tank you create a complex mix of sounds. Overflowing tanks and channels can easily be made from wood that will weather attractively as the water wears it.

In essence these are all variations of a waterfall, and the principle of collecting water at the lowest level of its journey and pumping it back to the highest allows for any number of visual and aural

ABOVE: *The Japanese are masters of the combination of water and sound. A simple bamboo spout draining water into a pot contains the essence of a waterfall.*

RIGHT: *This cascade combines the man-made control of a sequence of steps with the unharnessed power of a waterfall.*

OPPOSITE: *Water design at its most brilliant: a series of elegantly simple jets play into a long shallow canal at the gardens of Generalife in Granada, Spain.*

variations on this theme. The surface the water hits, be it pebbles, more water, wood, concrete, or whatever, will create the sound. Experiment with this. Work out what gives you most pleasure in that particular site and create the water feature around that.

Controlled jets make a much more tinkly sound. The marvelous jets lining the canal along the Patio de la Acequia at the Generalife in Granada or the Pathway of One Hundred Fountains at Villa d'Este just outside Rome are brilliant examples of this, but it can be done on a much smaller scale in a much smaller backyard. I have seen mini-jets surrounding a circular pond no bigger than 3 ft. (90 cm) in diameter. Each arc fell in the center of the pool and the ensemble was modulated by the wind, plucking at some jets and dispersing them, spreading and softening the sound.

Finally, you can use the power of water to create a hard sound. The Japanese have done this for centuries with a length of hollow bamboo balanced on a stand, called a *sozu*. The stem is closed at one end and water trickles into the other, open end. When it fills to a certain point, the bamboo tips forward, emptying its water, before swinging back again, clunking against the feed pipe as it does so. The hollow resonance of the bamboo makes a distinctive clacking sound which may serve to alarm and deter deer but is captivating to the human ear.

We can listen to wind ruffling through grasses, leaves, a piece of paper jerking across the lawn, poppy heads swaying gently

Every wind will make variations in sound— from the delicate rustle of a calm summer's day to the agonized rattle that sends leaves streaming to the ground. From left to right: a young Norway maple has large lobed leaves that flutter in their spring softness; silver birches are the first to trap any wind, which they seem to shake from themselves; and beech leaves in autumnal dryness rustle like parchment.

WIND

When I was a child I slept in an attic room right up in the branches of a huge beech tree. There was something immensely comforting about lying snug in bed listening to the heaving branches and the leaves flapping and pattering against the house on a windy autumnal night. Now, as an adult in similar circumstances, I always make a mental checklist of any trees that might not be supported properly, any windows left open in the greenhouse, or any elongated soft growth in midsummer that is

—and we can differentiate between the sounds.

liable to be damaged by winds. The sound of wind in the middle of the night sets me gardening in my head.

Wind is the primary driver of sound in the garden, carrying and making it, everything having its own tune when brushed by the wind. If the wind is blowing at a constant speed, without any pressure changes or obstructions, it is as soundless as it is invisible. But when it gusts and, even more significantly, when it meets a surface, it creates sound. That surface might be the ground, a roof, a solitary leaf on an expanse of lawn, or the

massed branches of a woodland in winter. All create subtle variations in sound that are quite distinctive to the human ear.

Grasses catch the wind and sigh, and the dried seedheads of herbaceous plants whistle. Spring leaves are silkily sibilant, like young girls rustling in new party dresses. As the same leaves dry out in autumn their sound becomes more brittle and rattles rather than whispers. Willows rustle like a grass skirt and birches shake the wind out of themselves. In a strong wind pines whoosh and roar like waves crashing on a distant shore.

Just occasionally leaves sound in perfect stillness. I have heard oak leaves clatter like plates dropping on a stone floor as they fall to the ground after a heavy frost on an absolutely still autumn day. It is the sound of a door closing finally on the season.

But most autumnal leaves rattle and rustle to the ground in a vague way, flicking off the branches into a high wind, streaming down on a clear, gusty autumn day and drifting dissolutely in a light breeze. Fallen leaves jostle around the garden until they are collected or become too sodden to move, and their ragged sound is an integral part of gardening. Instead of seeing them as litter to be collected and turned into leaf mold, we should first enjoy the sound they make.

You can plant to catch the wind. Grasses do this best, with their long stems and feathery heads whose skeletons last through the winter. The wind seems to shuffle through them. The range is large, from the gigantic bamboos (which are simply woody grasses) such as *Bambusa multiplex*, which grows to 49 ft. (15 m), down to the tiny squirreltail grass (*Hordeum jubatum*), growing only to a maximum of 2 ft. (60 cm). The genus *Miscanthus* has seventeen different species, all tall and stately. *Miscanthus sinensis* is the most commonly grown, with a number of good varieties, including the pink-feathered *M.s.* 'Kleine Fontane', which is suitable for small gardens, reaching only 4 ft. (1.2m), and *M.s.* 'Silberfeder', which grows to 6 ft. (1.8 m) and has silvery plumes. Many gardeners are familiar with what is rather loosely called "pampas grass" (which is more often a species such as *Cortaderia selloana* from New Zealand, nowhere near the South American

ABOVE: *Grasses catch and trap the wind, which constantly smoothes and flattens them just like sand dunes, creating a distinctive shuffling, sifting sound.*

pampas) growing in isolated clumps on the margins of lawns.

Grasses do not need to be planted as individual specimens but can be integrated into the mixed planting of a border, although some grasses, like *Glyceria maxima* 'Variegata' will spread voraciously. I made the mistake of

planting this in a herbaceous border, where it tried to take over the entire plot. It is now relegated to the wild garden, where it looks much better. In winter the 3 ft. (90 cm) stems sway in the wind with a sound like rustling silk. Most grasses will tolerate dry conditions, although they also need sun to do well.

However, moor grass (*Molina caerulea*), which reaches 2 ft. (60 cm), will grow in wet spots and looks especially good against a dark background.

Never cut back the stems and leaves of any grass in autumn, as it deprives the plant of insulating properties over winter as well as denying the gardener its idiosyncratic, wind-blown song. Cut this old material down to the ground in early spring instead, to allow the vivid new growth to take over.

In principle I am opposed to cutting back any growth until spring. This might offend against the unsensuous gardener's sense of order, but it adds much to the range of winter sound. Two of my favorites are the seed pods of poppies, which tap against each other like skulls on poles, and the transparent medallions of honesty, like paper rattles.

Constant wind drives strong men mad. Just as there is no stillness, there is also no silence, no restfulness to be found anywhere. But wind can be baffled by hedges, trees, and shrubs, enabling you to create a controlled balance of sound that soothes rather than maddens. A deciduous hedge is far more effective against wind than a wall; the wind breaks up as it passes through the branches of the hedge while it is merely lifted over the wall, coming down even harder on the leeward side. The sound of the wind is dispersed through a hedge; the roar becomes a lullaby of distant waves meeting rocks, comforting in the same way as that beech outside my window when I was a child.

ABOVE: *The beautiful seed heads of poppies rattle in the wind, first with seeds inside and then, after these have been spread, one against the other, making two quite different types of sound.*
LEFT: *Rushes have an unusual combination of soft featheriness and a harsh brittle noise as their dry stems jostle one with another.*

BIRDS AND INSECTS

A garden without birdsong is an abandoned place. No gardener who has stepped outside at dawn on a spring morning (and every sensuous gardener should step that way as often as they can) can fail to appreciate the manner in which the dawn chorus enriches their perception of the place.

Even in the middle of the city a garden provides the ideal habitat for many birds. There are the songbirds like the song thrush, becoming alarmingly reduced in numbers but still gracing the top of the tallest tree in many gardens at dawn and dusk, singing fit to break your heart with its repeated refrain.

The wood thrush is known for singing at dawn and dusk, especially in spring. Carolina wrens, robins, orioles, catbirds, and cardinals all insistently stake their territory through their song.

These songbirds dominate our interpretation of the airwaves, although just as important and more frequent are the chatterings, beeps, mewings, snatches of song, and shrill alarms of other birds such as starlings, swallows, sparrows, wrens, finches, and titmice.

I recall switching on the radio and hearing the most exquisite burbling birdsong pouring out to me. I was moved to tears, bewitched. It turned out that this exotic song belonged to the most common bird in the British Isles, the humble wren, and what I was hearing was its normal high twitterings slowed down sixteen times, revealing the true beauty and complexity of the song. It made me realize that we hear only a fraction of the music around us.

It does not stop at dusk. Above my own garden the curlews call like lost souls all the spring nights long and owls can often be heard in town gardens with mature trees nearby.

Of course birds do not tenant gardens because of the aesthetics. They are after the rich food supply that they provide, and to get the most out of birdsong one has to understand that food chain. There are two main sources of bird food in a garden: vegetable and animal. The former is made up of seeds, fruit, and berries, and the latter of insects, caterpillars, slugs, and worms. Clearly this group is enormously beneficial to the garden and every effort should be made to encourage them.

All the birds that we now find commonly in a garden originate from woodland, and the nearer that your garden approximates to this original habitat, the happier the birds will be. In towns, gardens are an oasis of vegetation and as important to the birds as a water source is to the desert traveler.

This does not mean that you have to make a garden that is only a collection of tall trees interspersed with undergrowth, because woodland is so varied that it encompasses every possible style of garden. But it does mean that you have to avoid too much tidiness. Tidiness is the worst enemy to wildlife of all kinds, as well as to creativity in the garden. Never use insecticides, slugbait, or any form of pesticide, and allow sufficient cover to develop for the birds to nest in. Seedheads should be left on plants until they have all fallen or been eaten. This is particularly important at the end of summer when birds are building up reserves for winter. It also means leaving dead branches and even trees to stand, as they provide ideal breeding sites for grubs and insects to breed in.

What one is after is a self-regulating balance within what is a very unnatural environment. No one insect can ever get out of hand if there are predators to consume the excess but, by the

same token, no predators can exist where they have nothing to predate on. So one has to strive to maintain a healthy balance.

A significant pay-off from this policy—other than a healthy, uncontaminated garden, which should be reason enough—is the added sound that insects make. Where there are flowers you are bound to have the hum, buzz, whine, and drone of insects raiding pollen. Best of all are bees, whose busyness is such a calmative. Wasps are the Angry Brigade of the garden, their buzz as aggressive as the bee's is bumbly. I associate wasps as much with a petulant zizz in a jam jar on a table in the garden as with their black and yellow stripes.

All the pale, night-scented flowers rely mainly on moths to pollinate them, and the furry flap and bump of moths stumbling into flowers, leaves, and you in the dark is all part of the garden's rich soundscape.

OPPOSITE: *An English robin fiercely defies all intruders with its clear, sweet spring song.*
ABOVE: *By leaving a vegetative debris, you provide seeds and insects for birds, like this bluebird, to feed on in winter. In return they will sing for their supper.*

HUMAN SOUNDS

Gardens are for people, and a sensuous aspect of the garden that seems rarely to be considered is the sound of the gardener at work. A garden can be the perfect marriage between nature and mankind, but we are often coy about the gardener's daily involvement in creating and maintaining this unnatural slice of tightly controlled outdoors. Even the most seemingly "natural" gardens entail constant hours of primping and adjustment to maintain the artifice of their naturalness.

I love the sound of this human activity in the garden. I love the clink of a steel spade on a stone as its handler turns the soil. I like the drone of a lawnmower in the hazy distance and the squeaking wheels of a wheelbarrow being pushed toward the compost heap. The sound that a rake makes as it is drawn across the ground in the repetitive process of gathering fallen leaves is part of the patchwork of sensuous associations of a gardener's autumn. Even a rake pushed through the refining tilth makes a sound as it combs the soil. There is a satisfying sucking, pulling noise as heavy soil lifts from virgin earth in a clod, and a soft absorption when the spade slides into richly cultivated ground.

The sound of shears clicking and snipping at topiary or hedging is the sound of focused industry akin to the tapping of a sculptor's chisel. It signifies honorable labor and that always has an unpretentious dignity. But for most people the sound they are most aware of is the mechanical whine of a mower, strimmer, hedgecutter, or cultivator coming from a neighboring garden. This is perhaps the most radical change in gardening. We tolerate sounds we would rather not hear because of the gains in speed and efficiency. But it is salutary to remember the advantages to the mind of the rhythm of man and hand tool, replacing the incessant drive of mechanical sound with human activity.

We are all used to the tapping of heels on pavements, but the "hard" areas of the garden have their own sounds. The most obvious of these is gravel, which is marketed for its security value by virtue of the crunching noise it makes when walked over. But every surface creates a different noise when walked on, wheeled over, or even scuffed as chairs are adjusted, be it the jiggling bumps of cobbles, the crunch of gravel, or the muffled, hollow sound of bricks. Each distinctive sound becomes associated with that piece of the garden. We hardly ever stop and think about it, but if we were blind, then this awareness of an area by its aural qualities would be pushed forward and become vital.

Finally there is the best sound of all in a garden: the laughter of children. If the garden is fun and if there is opportunity for adults and children alike to play, laughter will never be far away.

Go, said the bird, for the leaves were full of children,
Hidden excitedly, containing laughter.
Go, go, go, said the bird: human kind
Cannot bear very much reality.
T.S. ELIOT, 'BURNT NORTON'

OPPOSITE: *The sound of raking leaves is only meaningful in repetition. Each draw of the rake accumulates the awareness of the season.*
ABOVE: *"Footfalls echo in the memory." Frosty grass crunches like gravel as you walk on it.*

TASTE

For too long vegetable gardening

has been obsessed with shape and size.

Better that care be lavished from tilth

to table on growing tasty food whose

beauty is a byproduct to be relished.

ABOVE: *Peas snapped from the plant and eaten from the pod have an*

irresistible raw green sweetness.

ABOVE: *Ordinary vegetables can be extraordinarily beautiful. Sunlight is cupped in the leaves of young cabbage (top), and embryonic peas in the pod are revealed by the light of a spring morning (bottom).*
OPPOSITE: *Growing food—be it herbs, fruit, or vegetables—is the most intimate form of gardening, and creates the most personal of gardens.*

EVEN WITH OUR SENSES FINELY HONED, *we are all very bad at describing tastes. Our language is superbly equipped for visual analysis but clumsy for most of the other senses. Taste is also an internal, subjective thing. We are too influenced by what tastes nice or nasty to be objective about what it tastes like. The best we can do is to categorize a few universal tastes, although there is no scientific basis for this. It is generally—if arbitrarily— agreed that there are four reliable taste stimuli: salt, sweet, bitter, and sour. As early as the fourth century the Chinese had codified their tastes to include these four and a fifth: spicy— which might be better described as "hot" and which would include such foods as chilies, rocket, horseradish, and mustard. I know of nothing that can be grown in the garden whose taste can be described as salty, and therefore that category of taste is not covered in this book.*

Caring as much as we do about the details of the food we put in our mouths, it seems strange that we should be so much less careful about the food we pull from our garden. There is often an atmosphere of celebration, a kind of secular harvest festival, for having grown anything at all, without the critical rigor most people apply to the kitchen.

Men are mostly to blame. In primitive societies vegetable growing is left to the women, who are also expected to cook them. There is therefore an inbuilt relationship between horticulture and gastronomy. The meal begins at least with the seed, if not at the initial cultivation of the ground. It puts vegetable growing somewhere between farming and herb growing; utilitarian but on a small scale. But then men muscled into the kitchen garden without setting foot in the kitchen. This is an aspect of the male obsession with order and control that I touched upon in the Introduction. The male influence meant that vegetable and fruit growing began to be measured and valued by size and quantity, rather than by quality. This view still seems to predominate. Visit any flower show and the fruit and vegetables section is still judged entirely by the look and scale of the produce without any reference to taste whatsoever.

Having said that, until twenty years ago most cooks rigorously boiled all taste and texture out of any vegetable, whatever its size, serving a uniform, tasteless, soggy mush. So perhaps sizeism was a passing compensation for the ultimate destruction of all the virtues of the vegetable on the plate and on the palate. But in those twenty-five years we in the West have absorbed many other culinary cultures. Every supermarket now supplies the ingredients for a range of global cuisines. The problem is that supermarkets sell their wares by looks, not by taste. You are quite likely to see the perfect tomato, exquisite eggplants, mouth-watering pears, but the chance of tasting more than blandly familiar wateriness is much more remote.

This schism between what fruit and vegetables look like as they grow and as they end up on the table is entirely irrelevant for the modern gardener with little time or space to get into the full-scale machismo of conventional kitchen gardening.

FOOD IN THE GARDEN

Everything tastes better outdoors. Everything tastes *more* outdoors. It is as if the openness of air, sky, and frondescence opens out our taste buds and allows us to savor food fully.

Flavor is not the same as taste, even though many of us use the two words synonymously. Flavor is properly the combination of taste and scent. We have all experienced the blunting of our sense of taste when afflicted with a heavy cold; the more we are able to enjoy scents, the better we will savor the full flavor of food. When we eat outside we are exposed to a heady mix of scents that is accentuated and enriched by warm sun. All our senses are heightened and in consequence food is experienced more richly.

Simple, ordinary meals become feasts when eaten in the last warmth of a setting summer sun, surrounded by honeysuckle, tobacco plants, and night-scented stock, the air rich with the blackbirds' final song, and the meal concluded by pulling the ripe figs from the tree beneath which you sit. This is no unattainable fantasy: I speak from delicious experience of many such meals in a small inner-city garden.

It is also a mistake to confine the limits of al fresco eating with a restricted notion of what constitutes outdoor food. The barbecue has a lot to answer for here: burned sausages, cheap rubbery hamburgers, doughy buns, and a salad of tasteless tomato, iceberg lettuce, and hydroponically grown cucumbers do not make a memorable gastronomic experience. Bad food is not worth eating, however lovely the weather or situation. Far better to have *"A loaf of bread beneath the bough/A flask of wine, a book of verse—and Thou."* I have found that any food, from a stew to bread and jam, is eminently suitable for an outdoor meal. Simply carry it out on a tray to the garden table. The process of cooking

outside is fun, though, and the smells and anticipation of the food as it cooks heighten the pleasure of the meal.

Too often we eat in the garden on a paved surface, sitting on chairs with unsensuous textures such as plastic or metal, and surrounded by the house or walls. Try eating in the middle of the lawn or beneath a tree; treat the meal like a picnic, an adventure rather than a ritual. All your senses will rise to the occasion.

OPPOSITE: *All food tastes better outdoors and the simplest meal becomes a memorable occasion when eaten in a beautiful garden.*
ABOVE: *The brilliance of golden, plum, and beef tomatoes contrasts against the purple inkiness of eggplants and capsicums.*

Simple, ordinary meals become feasts when eaten in the last warmth of a setting summer sun.

TYPES OF TASTE

Sweet

Until the introduction of sugarcane from the Americas in the seventeenth century, most people had only the natural sweetness in foods with the precious addition of honey. Nevertheless, sweetmeats were a delicacy for the rich and Elizabeth I's famous black teeth are a testimony to the irresistible allure of sweetness to those who had access to it.

Of course we need sugars in order to survive. Our bodies digest the more complex carbohydrates into sugar and store them in the liver and in muscle tissue as glycogen. Any vigorous exercise depends upon glycogen as an immediate fuel supply. Most people are familiar with the concept of "low blood sugar" (properly hypoglycemia, referring to the glucose level in the blood; diabetes is the opposite condition when there is too high a glucose level) and the hit of energy that sugars will give you when in this state. But we want much, much more than we need. One of the reasons that we will happily ingest so much sugar is that we have a very crude awareness of sweet tastes. Most people are unable to detect sweetness at a level below one part in two hundred. This means that high levels of sugar can be "hidden" in foods and the food processing industry has used this to make the most tasteless foods more desirable by loading them with sugar.

The secret of combining subtle flavors with sweetness is warmth. The best place to "store" food is on the plant that bears it. It is only by eating herbs, fruit, and vegetables as soon as possible after picking that we can we enjoy their truest and best taste. All other forms of food storage are designed solely to facilitate distribution and increase profits: tastiness is an advertiser's afterthought.

The plants we associate with sweetness are fruits. Fruits are sweet because they manufacture fructose—a simple and easily digested form of sugar. It is the sweetest of all sugars and is broken down more slowly than glucose, so is better at providing sustained energy.

Plants rely on the conversion of sunlight to sugar—via the process of photosynthesis—to survive. We have learned to nurture those plants that store up large amounts of this sugar for their future survival and harvest them before they themselves draw upon their starch reserve. All the root vegetables are excellent examples of this, with the potato being the most common and the parsnip perhaps the best example of sugar stored as starch.

We associate sweetness with ripeness and fruition. The "fruits" of the garden are sweet not just in taste but also in manner and implication. Sweetness in the mouth comes as a reward and a measure of the perfect moment, the perfect taste—not sickly sweet, which would signify overripeness, yet with none of the unyielding sourness that would mean it was not ready. This ideal sweetness can be found in a hundred fruits and vegetables, from peas peeled from the pod to new potatoes, whose perfect sweetness can be unlocked only by cooking.

Nevertheless, those occasional moments of perfect sweetness in the garden override any theory. At such moments plants exist solely for our pleasure. And what pleasure there is to be had! Sweet tastes are as much a luxury as they have ever been, despite the modern ubiquitousness of sugar. Anyone who has picked a ripe strawberry from the warm earth and bitten into its juicy, honey sweetness knows this. There are peaches to be eaten warm from the brick of the wall they are grown against, tomatoes waiting to release their own musty, musky sweetness as teeth break their skin, dusty figs that split apart between the thumbs in almost unbearable voluptuousness, baby carrots pulled from the warm soil, swished under a tap and crunched by the dozen. The garden holds a voluptuary sweetness that no supermarket can match.

Sour

Sourness is not found in any vegetable and in only a few mature fruits. It is usually a signal of unripeness, so we instinctively reject the food as inedible.

But there are exceptions. The most obvious is the lemon. For many people this is the defining taste of sourness, although lemons do vary enormously, from mouth-shriveling sour to deliciously sweet. In wet, temperate climates the cooking apple takes on the lemon's role as the arbiter of sourness. Many apples can be eaten raw, but some, such as 'Bramley's Seedling', are only edible if cooked, when they turn into a sweet sauce. Varieties such as 'Duchess of Oldenburg' and 'Northern Spy' are suitable for pies, as they retain their consistency when cooked.

Crab apples were used for verjuice before lemons became available. This is really a form of cider vinegar and was used to make pickles or to curdle milk for cheese-making.

Red- and blackcurrants were unknown in the ancient world and one reason for this is that they need plenty of sugar—which was rare and expensive—to make them palatable. It is extraordinary how powerful is the rich, almost pungent sourness of currants against a sweet companion. The British dessert called summer pudding is the most delicious example of this. Of anything the garden can offer the palate, summer pudding is the most sublime. I can smell one now, see its firm consistency on the plate, dribbling a rich red, the white bread bruised with juice. Redcurrants are probably the easiest of all fruit to grow,

OPPOSITE: *Raspberries are the most delicious soft fruits; unlike strawberries, they are never bland, their sweetness being tinged with a dash of sour.*
BELOW: *Endive is one of the few garden tastes that is identifiably bitter. These blanched heads will add an extra dimension of taste to any salad.*

tolerating cold, wet shade and recovering strongly from any amount of inexpert pruning.

Damson plums are the most direct link between domesticated and wild fruit, which means that breeders have found them hard to "improve." They can be eaten raw, but only in the short period between ripeness and rottenness. Cooking extends their eating season and is what they are best for, making rich jams and pies.

Morello cherries are inedibly sour until cooked, but once boiled they are delicious in pies, tarts, or jelly, or as a sauce with game. They have much the same needs as pears, and will tolerate wetter, colder conditions than apples or sweet cherries; and they will grow perfectly well on a cold, north-facing wall.

Bitter

Bitterness is the easiest taste to detect: most people can spot one part in two million and we reject it instinctively, with a puckering of the mouth that is a health warning, suggesting that the food might do us harm. But if food was all sweetness and light, it would be like a garden filled only with pink and white flowers; however individually lovely, the overall effect would be too much of a good thing. We need another edge to taste, just as we need shade and darkness of color in the borders.

Bland lettuce is always improved by a dash of bitter leaves. The coarse outer leaves of a normal cos lettuce will often taste bitter and are nearly always rejected because of this. I remember

plate for a week or so after they have matured, they grow white and sweet. I would argue that this wastes the best thing about them, namely their bitterness.

Endive is a perennial, although it is always grown as an annual. There are many different types, of which the most common is Witloof endive. You treat it like lettuce, sowing in late spring and early summer and letting it develop throughout the season. Dig the plants up in late autumn, trim off the leaves, and fit the roots fairly tightly—two or three together—in a pot of old potting mix or sand. Water them lightly and put another pot over the top, blocking out all light. Keep them in a warmish place and the white "chicons" will grow in a few weeks.

Radicchio is another type of pleasantly bitter chicory. This starts out green and reddens as the leaves turn in to form a crisp, sweeter heart. The very hardy 'Treviso' type does not form a heart but is able to withstand frost and provides a wonderful intense winter color.

Sorrel is rarely grown in gardens now, which is a pity since its bitterness is piquant and delicious. It is as good cooked or made into a sharp sauce as it is raw in a salad. There are two types, the large-leafed, which is an "improved" version of wild sorrel (*Rumex acetosa*), and French sorrel (*R. scutatus*), which has smaller, round leaves like watercress. The latter likes a well-drained position and the former rich, moist soil. Exposure to hot sun will dramatically increase the bitterness, making it unpalatable.

Although broad beans are full of starchy sweetness, their skin is bitter and grows increasingly so as it ages. The secret is to eat broad beans very young, before the skin has a chance to thicken and spoil the buttery sweetness of the bean itself, otherwise you are faced with skinning every single bean.

LEFT TO RIGHT: *Lemons (left) are the definitive sour taste for many people, although they are rarely as sour as unripe damsons (center). Chili peppers (right) fall into the category of "hot" tastes.*

long ago seeing rows of cos lettuce tied up as they matured to reduce the bitterness of their outside leaves, but breeders have developed plants with a greater natural sweetness since then, making this sight a rarity.

Endives and chicory are the easiest plants to grow that will add a dimension of bitterness to a salad; although quite different in appearance, they are in fact from the same family. Almost every seed catalogue sells curly-leafed chicory, which grows like lettuce but has a distinctive white base and inner leaves, and a much denser leaf habit. The exterior, green leaves are much more bitter than the white, interior ones. If you tie the plants up with string to deprive them of light, or cover them with an inverted

TOP FRUIT

Top fruit is the innocently self-congratulatory name given to fruits grown on trees such as apples, pears, plums, damson plums, medlars, mulberries, apricots, peaches, cherries, and quinces.

What an extraordinary range of taste there is in that list! There are over two thousand varieties of apple alone, each with a definable flavor. If you devoted a lifetime to the epicurean exploration of orchard fruits, from the musky sweetness of apricots to the almost rotting edge of "bletted" medlars, you would still be discovering new tastes well into your old age.

Apples can be bought anywhere in the West. The chances are, however, that even with a satisfying texture, they will taste of very little. It therefore makes sense to grow only those varieties that have good taste, are impossible to buy, or that do not keep. For commercial reasons the two groups overlap. I will give just

two examples. 'Cox's Orange Pippin' fulfills most expectations of the perfect apple. At its best it is nutty, sweet, and just slightly piquant. Pure joy. But it is a very temperamental tree—hard to grow, hard to crop—and hates the cold, wet weather of much of Britain and northern North America. A supermarket Cox, although often less than perfect, is likely to be much better than any you can grow at home. 'Golden Delicious', meanwhile, has become the epitome of the bland, tasteless, cheap fruit, and yet if it is grown in the sunny, warm location it prefers and allowed to ripen properly on the tree, it is a delicious, honey-sweet apple. It does not keep for long when it is ripe, however, so what you buy is usually a travesty of the true fruit.

The pear is the most sensuous of all the fruits. Fulsome, with rounded, firm body, the ripe flesh is nectar sweet and juicy as you bite into it. It is the perfect celebration of all the senses, the

OPPOSITE: '*Egremont Russet*' *apples glowing like golden orbs. Russets are rare in orchards, although* '*Roxburg Russet*' *survives for home gardens.*

RIGHT: *It is best to pick pears before they fall or are attacked by insects, carefully monitoring them as they ripen indoors. But your trouble is worth it for there are few pleasures in life to equal biting into the succulent flesh of a perfectly ripe pear.*

BELOW: *There are more than two thousand varieties of apple, each with an idiosyncratic taste and appearance, and most, like this* '*Fiesta*', *as decoratively beautiful on the tree as they are tasty.*

BELOW RIGHT: *The pear* '*Durondeau*' *in glorious maturity, ripe in body as well as taste.*

sensuous made sensual. To enjoy a pear at its best you must pick it unripe and allow it to reach the ideal moment in storage. It is not easy judging when this is. Prodding it with a rude thumb is hopelessly brutal, and will bruise any fruit that is ripe. I tend to go on a mixture of signals, combining smell—an almost alcoholic whiff of sweetness; color, where a good flush of yellow is a sign of maturity; and feel, especially of the stem which, when the fruit is really ripe, should resist slightly and then plop out. It is always a gamble, but I suppose this only adds to the undiluted joy of a perfect pear.

The plum family, including gages and damson plums, is rather old-fashioned. Until the age of the home freezer these fruits were an important part of the rural household pantry cupboard because they could be kept so well in jars and as jelly, although this did mean extra work preparing them. Being small, they were also a little more labor-intensive to collect. But it is a pity not to persevere with them, if only for the pleasure of the uncooked fruit from the tree. The variety of types of plums is enormous, but my own favorite is the greengage. Small, with almost transparent flesh of an exceptional sweetness when ripe, it is a rarely grown delight.

Damson plums have been largely ignored by modern breeders. Because they come true from seed, the fruit from a tree in your garden tastes exactly the same as the fruit the crusaders brought back from Damascus eight hundred years ago. Damson jam is the richest and best and damson cheese is good with lamb or game as well as bread and butter.

Peaches are a perfect example of a specific combination of senses producing a memory. The gentle fuzz of a peach skin grazes the lips before we bite into it and it is this texture, followed milliseconds later by an explosion of syrupy taste that is peachy. A peach *must* be eaten fresh from the tree: it will hardly keep more than a day; any bruising will rot it and picked under-ripe it has fraction of its flavor. But get the timing right and it is blissful.

OPPOSITE: *Sweet cherries are a delicious midsummer treat, not just because of their taste but for their voluptuous shape and texture. Morello cherries are easier to grow but better eaten cooked.*
LEFT: *Greengages are very similar in appearance to small plums but, to my mind, they are superior in taste. They need a drier, warmer summer than plums if they are to ripen well.*

ABOVE: *Peaches growing against an old brick wall, protected by it. To thrive, peach trees need a very particular set of conditions: lots of moisture, rich, well-drained soil, cold winters, and hot summers. If this mixture can be provided, they will respond with large crops of fruit.*

ABOVE: *Blackberries swollen like the pumped muscles of a bodybuilder. They are grown on a large scale in the Pacific Northwest and can also be picked in local meadows and by country roads.* OPPOSITE: *Blueberries and their cousin the bilberry have a distinctive tartly sweet, slightly smoky flavor that makes them instantly recognizable. They grow well in acid soil— wherever heathers and rhododendrons flourish.*

SOFT FRUIT

Soft fruit is the term for fruits that grow on bushes or plants near the ground. All berries, be they strawberries, raspberries, loganberries, tayberries, gooseberries, blackberries, blueberries, bilberries, or cranberries, and with the notable exception of the mulberry, are soft fruit, as are the currants, black, white, and red.

Strawberries are the best known, most eaten, and most overestimated soft fruit. Most bought strawberries taste of little more than a squishy sweetness. If you want to eat strawberries that taste as good as folklore still insists—despite the chilled imposters dished up for dessert at any eating establishment at all times of the year—you must grow your own, wait until high summer, and eat them as they should be eaten, still warm from the sun.

Your soil type is likely to be the major determining factor for the taste of your strawberries. A light and sandy soil is usually favored by the commerical growers as it will produce an earlier crop, but the richer and heavier the soil, the better the flavor.

Strawberries can easily be grown in a container. You can invest in a special planter which has cupped holes in the sides that you plant through Alternatively you may prefer to cultivate the small but especially delicious alpine strawberry (*Fragaria alpina*), which fruits constantly from early summer through to mid-autumn, in a large pot or windowbox. It is far better, surely, to have one small, exquisite bowl a year than a mountain of travesties.

The choicest strawberry is nowhere nearly as good as an average raspberry. A dish of the deep pink fruits freshly picked from the garden, lightly sprinkled with sugar, and served with plenty of light cream (it needs to be light to get the smooth white flow over the knobbly red surface of the fruits), eaten outside on a warm evening with a glass of cold, fruity white wine is one of the greatest treats the garden has to offer.

Raspberries like wet, cool growing conditions. There are two types, the summer-fruiting varieties, which crop in midsummer, and the autumn-fruiting, which crop from late summer until the first frosts.

Gooseberries will also grow happily in cool, moist conditions as long as they can get some sun to ripen. Gooseberry fool is the food of the gods, with gooseberry jam and gooseberry tart running close behind. And hot gooseberry sauce poured over freshly caught grilled mackerel.... Gooseberries need a high level of potash, so give them a potash feed (potassium sulfate or rock potash) in early spring and mulch well with compost or manure.

Currants can be divided into two groups: blackcurrants and the rest, even though they are all of the same *Ribes* genus. Blackcurrants flower on young wood, whereas red and white currants flower on the previous season's growth. If ever one needs an active description of flavor, that combination of aroma and taste, pop a blackcurrant into your mouth. It is tart, almost unpleasant, but the unforgettable smell and taste linger long in the memory, rising to sublime heights in the jams and jellies—not to mention summer pudding—that are the real fruits of the currant bush.

LEFT: *Strawberries (above) are best still warm with sunshine. Too often they are served cold and out of season, tasting of bland mush. Most gooseberries (below) need cooking but are always worth the trouble for their distinctive piquancy.*
OPPOSITE: *Dangling like glass beads, redcurrants are essential ingredients of summer pudding and, as a jelly, the perfect accompaniment to lamb or game.*

GROWING VEGETABLES

The only good reason for growing anything edible in the garden is a combination of freshness and taste. Yet this is reason enough, because with many vegetables it is the *only* way to capture the true freshness and fullness of taste. It follows that the edible gardening process must begin at the table and work its way back via the kitchen to the garden, rather than the other, more conventional way around. Grow what you want to see ending up on your plate, not what happens to flourish in the garden or allotment. To this end it obviously makes sense to grow food that spends as short a time as possible between garden and table. Your garden is the best and quickest supply of fast food there is: fast food that is tailored and nurtured to satisfy your own idiosyncratic and seasonal tastes.

Conventional gardening has the vegetable garden filled with as wide a range of vegetables as possible, but divided into three main groups: Roots (turnips, carrots, rutabagas, parsnips, beets), Brassicas (cabbages, cauliflowers, brussel sprouts, broccoli) and Legumes (peas and beans). Tomatoes, celery, spinach, onions, and leeks are traditionally grown with this legume group, and salad crops are grown wherever space will allow. These three groups are rotated annually to prevent disease and to cater for their different manuring requirements.

The modern gardener can largely ignore these conventions. The incidental salad crops are likely to be their prime concern and should take the lion's share of space, although smaller vegetables invariably taste more intense than their bigger counterparts. By growing plants closer together and harvesting them younger, you not only need less space but also get a quality of food that cannot be bought in any shop.

The principle of succession within one crop—typically lettuce—and between different types of vegetables, based upon a sowing of a small amount of seed every few weeks rather than an entire pack at a time, gives a steady supply of the food that you have chosen, that most satisfies your tastebuds and for which absolute freshness is at a premium.

OPPOSITE: *Looking like the giant orange offspring of tomato and melon, pumpkins make superb eating, store well, and are as much a symbol of autumn as falling leaves.*

ABOVE LEFT: *Potatoes are traditionally the staple crop of the gardener; these are sweet potatoes which are better suited to tropical conditions.*

ABOVE RIGHT: *Tomatoes were originally golden; their familiar redness is a result of hybridization.*

LEFT: *Fast food: nothing is easier—or more satisfying—than gathering the ingredients for a salad from your garden minutes before a meal.*

Think of the whole process, from soil to table, as the preparation of a delicious meal.

SMALL-SCALE VEGETABLES

There are few gardens so small that they cannot provide the materials for a dish or two. Think of the whole process, from soil to table, as the preparation of a delicious meal. It makes gardening into exquisite foreplay. You nurture the plants, gently enticing them into the perfect pitch of ripeness, before leading them into the kitchen and subtly preparing them before consummation. The links between the ultimate site of fulfillment, a table—preferably outdoors—and the stages of horticultural seduction, through choosing varieties, planting, feeding, thinning, protecting against birds, picking, and cooking, are all unbreakably forged.

One of the secrets of small-scale vegetable gardening is very simple: do not grow large vegetables! By selecting plants that take up little room—like tomatoes, carrots, salad crops, and radishes—and by cropping them while they are much smaller than convention dictates, you will create the space to grow a range of plants.

Only grow what you cannot easily buy and always choose varieties for their taste rather than for their cropping prowess. You are able to grow a surprising range of tastes in a limited space, from the sweetness of carrots, parsnips, baby turnips, and beets the size of golf balls to baby cauliflowers, every kind of bean and lettuce, as well as small but practical onions, shallots, leeks, and garlic.

Intensity of taste with a baby carrot or young broad bean can be matched directly by intensity of organization within the available growing space. By growing your crops not in rows but in small blocks and grids about 5 ft. (1.5 m) square, you make everything accessible from the edges and ensure that every usable inch of ground is being productive. The other tip is to grow your vegetables upward. Grow beans up a tripod of poles in a pot; grow peas up against a wall; use grow bags on a hard surface to grow any shallow-rooting plants such as tomatoes, French beans, cucumbers, or sweet corn.

An intelligent use of the law of succession will avoid the glut/dearth that seems to hit any vegetable garden at some stage of the year. The trick is to sow small quantities at short intervals. A packet of lettuce seed, for example, will make four sowings; spacing them at ten-day intervals ensures a steady but not overwhelming supply of fresh and tasty food that is always to your taste.

Salad crops, which can be collected and eaten within the same five minutes, are always the most satisfactory for a small garden. Great big lettuces usually have tiny little tastes. It is better to grow smaller plants, allowing one or even two lettuces per person. Varieties such as 'Little Gem' (cos) or 'Tom Thumb' (butterhead) are ideal for this. Even if you have lots of space, loose-leaf lettuce is useful; in restricted conditions it is invaluable. They can be picked selectively—a handful of leaves from one plant—without damaging the remainder. They tend to bolt less easily than other types of lettuce and will regrow after picking. 'Salad Bowl' or 'Lollo Rosso' are two well-known varieties.

All these crops are easy to grow. They are cheap, instant, and can be raised in some permutation or other in anything from a single pot to a windowbox or a patch of border. Seen in this light, growing vegetables becomes altogether less intimidating. Anyone with a love of delicious food can do it.

OPPOSITE: *It is surprising how wide a range of vegetables can be grown in a small garden while still being productive and looking good.*
BELOW: *Runner beans are ideal for even the tiniest garden because they grow vertically and will perform well in a large pot. Even a small crop from just a few plants is a treat.*

DECORATIVE FRUIT AND VEGETABLES

There is a centuries-old tradition in English cottage gardens to grow flowers at random among the vegetables, creating a gorgeously unregulated jumble of color, form, and essential food. But in most contemporary gardens this is rare. We are accustomed to dividing our gardens into functional sections. While you are as likely to see a rose in the herb garden as you are fennel, angelica, or winter savory in the flower border, there is still some reticence about mixing vegetables and decorative planting. This is a shame, as many vegetables are wonderfully decorative in color and form. I am suggesting that a small garden could take on the spirit of cottage gardening—and grow vegetables, fruit, and herbs in among the flowers, deliberately combining all these elements for best effect.

Vegetables do not need to stand in straight lines or rows to flourish, and they do not need much space. The average urban back garden could add an interesting mix to the dinner table without sacrificing any visual effect to practicality. A short row of cos lettuce can be thinned after a few weeks and the thinnings replanted in among herbaceous plants and shrubs, as long as they are not completely shaded. Dwarf beans have pretty, pinkish purple flowers and the purple-podded variety follows these with wonderfully decorative pods. Runner

beans have more spectacular vermilion flowers that last and develop over a longer period and, like peas, can be grown very effectively against a trellis or even clambering over the back of another shrub. I grow yellow-podded as well as the purple variety and both have the necessary visual dash to contribute to the late summer garden.

Artichokes and cardoons are imposing vegetables with jagged-edged, glaucous gray leaves that grow to a huge size at the back of a border. They also sprout delicious, edible thistle heads.

Ruby chard, with its blood-red stems and veins underneath the crinkle-backed, purple-green leaves, is as dramatic as any ornamental foliage plant; it also acts as a foil for intense orange or purple flowers, such as California poppies or allium

heads. 'Cardinal' cabbage is a reddish purple and a superb foil in any border. A zany tennis ball of edible purple kohlrabi is a similar color.

Try dotting leeks between a range of tightly spaced plants in a border and letting them go to seed. Their typical allium seed heads will rise up to almost

6½ ft. (2 m) and be fully worthy of their place—although the leek will not be edible. I once let a whole bed of leeks go to seed and the mauve pompoms, balanced like giant upended mops, provided by far the most dramatic display in the garden for months.

Apples and pears are easily grown as espaliers, taking up little space and being one of the best ways of maximizing fruit production. Apricots and peaches can be fan-trained against a small wall space as long as it gets plenty of sun, and morello cherries can be grown in the same way against a cold, shady wall or fence.

Currants of every hue are easily as decorative as many of the more conventional inhabitants of a shrub border. Select varieties for their ornamental qualities, such as the wine-colored gooseberry 'Pink' or the pale pink greengage plum 'Pixwell', and you need not lose out on their primary function as suppliers of taste.

OPPOSITE ABOVE: *Kohlrabi is a kind of cabbage with the stem swelling into an edible corm. This is one of the more vividly decorative forms known as 'Purple Vienna'.*
OPPOSITE BELOW: *The distinctive immature flowers of the globe artichoke, which is one of the most striking of all vegetables.*

LEFT: *With its voluptuous and strongly veined leaves, red cabbage is handsome enough to grow in a border for its looks alone.*
ABOVE: *Although vegetables are usually grown in straight lines with their own imposed structure they always add a pleasant jumble to a garden, humanizing and softening it.*

HERBS IN THE SUN

Originally herbs were grown primarily as medicinal plants, with "pot herbs" being the culinary branch of the family used to add flavor and savor to a remorselessly bland diet. Nowadays, rather than blindly trusting herbal recipes, we prefer to be seduced by chemical formulae we do not understand. We tend to ignore the medical reaches of herbs, especially ones that have since acquired a strong culinary association, such as mint, garlic, or rosemary. However, there is a general assumption that herbs Do You Good and I suspect that their essential distinctiveness of taste contributes much to this view.

Most herbs are natives of Mediterranean regions with hot summers and dry winters, growing on thin, rocky soil. Consequently they perform best in our gardens on a poorly nourished, well-drained, light soil. Sunshine brings the oils to the surface of the leaves of sage, cilantro, rosemary, basil, oregano, and thyme and thus intensifies their taste as well as their scent and for this reason it is always best to give the sunniest part of the garden

to herbs rather than blindly obeying the oft-repeated dictum of planting culinary herbs near the back door—which might well be in deep shade.

Once upon a time all salad plants were categorized as "sallet herbs." Parsley, chives, basil, borage, lemon balm, salad burnet, caraway, chervil, lovage, marjoram, mint, sage, savory, tarragon, and thyme all add distinction to a salad (although perhaps not all at once). The secret is to gather a small handful absolutely fresh and sprinkle it on the salad, so that it enhances rather than dominates the flavor. My favorite fast food is a herb omelet made with newly laid eggs, and a salad made from whatever lettuces are ready in the garden sprinkled with lots of herbs, collected again on the basis of availability. The whole process—from hunger to fulfillment, including gathering the raw materials, cooking, presentation, and eating—takes no more than ten minutes.

With the exception of parsley, chives, and mint, all these herbs like as much sunshine as they can get and well-drained, poorish soil. Certain herbs that long for the sun will become lanky when

OPPOSITE: *Sage, marjoram, chives in flower, lavender, and thyme are grown in this plot in their own dedicated beds. Even when they are systematically controlled, herb gardens always look good in high summer.*

RIGHT: *Poppy seedheads mingle with fennel in flower. Poppies are ideal floral companions for herbs, liking the same sunny, well-drained conditions.*

BELOW: *Homegrown and freshly picked culinary herbs such as parsley and rosemary taste far better than anything you can buy in a supermarket.*

they are forced to grow in the shade. Hyssop is a good example; but if given an open, sunny spot it will grow fast and robustly, making an excellent low hedge. The leaves have a slightly bitter, almost minty taste, and are probably at their best with game, soups, or other rich, meaty dishes. The purple-flowering variety is most commonly seen, but it is available in white, too, as *Hyssopus officinalis* 'Alba'.

Basil (*Ocimum basilicum*) is perhaps the tenderest plant that most people will grow in their garden and thrives only in hot sunshine, yet it is essential for anyone even contemplating eating tomatoes (grown yourself, of course, eaten warm and zipping with flavor, rather than the chilled tasteless sort you get from the grocery). Purple basil (*O. b.* var. 'Purpurascens') looks wonderful both in the garden and on your plate, but has a less intense taste and is not so good for cooking.

Bay (*Laurus nobilis*) is the most physically robust of sun-loving herbs, making a large bush in cooler northern regions and a good-sized tree in its natural Mediterranean habitat. It will grow well in a container but must be brought indoors if the temperature drops below 23°F (–5°C) and remains there. The leaves can be used straight from the tree, adding a pungent dimension to the plainest stew or casserole.

HERBS IN THE SHADE

Not all herbs like hot, dry conditions. Even if your garden is shaded and the soil heavy, you can still grow a wide variety of herbs: parsley, angelica, comfrey, caraway, chervil, chives, fennel, feverfew, horseradish, all mints, sorrel, sweet cicely, bergamot, betony, and lemon balm all tolerate moist conditions. Lovage, bay, bistort, rue, salad burnet, sorrel, tansy, and yarrow will all grow in some degree of shade. As a rule of thumb, variegated or yellow varieties are better suited to shady sites.

Of all these, parsley, mint, and chives are the three that are most likely to be used on a daily basis. Parsley is notorious for being tricky to get going. There is a saying that where parsley grows well it is the man of the house who wears the trousers. My household has never had any trouble with parsley, but I suspect that it is due to our typical late sowings rather than my dominance in the trouser department. It grows better on heavier

soils, which are often slow to heat up in spring; it needs warm soil to germinate but a cool spot to grow well. It is this combination that causes problems. Parsley must always be kept well watered. Sowings at two-monthly intervals from late spring to early autumn will ensure a constant supply, even in winter. I prefer to use the flat-leaved variety whenever it is to be eaten raw, as it has a more intense flavor and is less gritty. The moss-leaved type is more common and excellent for cooking.

Mint prefers rich, moist conditions, but will grow almost anywhere and is almost impossible to get rid of once established, so keep it in a container or in a pot sunk in the ground. A good ruse is to knock the bottom out of an old metal bucket, which you then sink below the surface. The mint roots can grow as deep as they need to find moisture, but are less able to go sideways. There are many kinds of mint, but for cooking, apple mint (*Mentha suaveolens*), golden apple mint (*M.* x *gentilis*), spearmint (*M. spicata*), and lemon mint (*M. x piperata citrata*) are best. All should be used sparingly if they are not to dominate.

Chives (*Allium schoenoprasum*) are essential and will improve any salad. Although they have been cultivated in European gardens only since the sixteenth century, the Chinese have been using them since at least 3000 B.C. No plant is easier to grow and chives can be raised by the dozen from a single pack of seed. They like moist, rich soil but will cope with much less if need be. A healthy plant will give you four crops a year. Add chives to a cooked dish at the last minute, as the flavor disappears if it starts to cook through. And do not reject the purple flowers: they taste intensely oniony and look wonderful in a salad.

Horseradish (*Amoracia rusticana*) likes rich, deep soil that its enormous roots can sink into, but it is invasive and best relegated to a safety zone. Nevertheless, it is worth growing because sauce made from the freshly grated roots is better than anything you can buy, with a distinct sweetness and a familiar pepperiness.

If you want to dry herbs, pick them when their flavor is at its peak. Gather the leaves just before the flowers open; be sure they are dry when you do this. Dry them in the sun to retain the color, and store them in the dark to retain both color and flavor.

Taste is inextricably linked with health. We are an age obsessed with what we eat but never has the western world had

so much bad food to choose from. While no-one can tell you what you ought to enjoy, you can be confident that a diet based upon what you can reasonably grow in your garden will be healthy as well as delicious. The only drawback is that it spoils you: once you have eaten fruit, vegetables, and herbs grown for taste rather than appearance, picked in their prime, and consumed within hours of harvest, everyday bland supermarket fare will never again suffice.

OPPOSITE: *Chives and horseradish both enjoy a rich soil and will tolerate shade. Horseradish can become invasive once established, so is best contained, as here.*
ABOVE: *Bergamot (*Monarda didyma *'Cambridge Scarlet') is one of the floral highlights of any herb garden and its fragrance is a great attraction for bees.*
LEFT: *Angelica heads rise above light-fringed comfrey. Both plants relish damp conditions.*

SCENT

Every day we each draw about 23,000 breaths, dipping each time into a deep well of smells, almost all of which are confusing and unrecognizable.

ABOVE: *Honeysuckle (*Lonicera perciclymenum*) has a fragrance that is reliably attractive, but you would be hard put to say exactly why, or even to describe it at all.*

ABOVE: *The most exquisite natural fragrance is primarily a means of survival. The stronger the scent of a plant the greater is its attraction to pollinators and the more likely that it will breed and ensure the survival of its species.*
OPPOSITE: *Insects that are attracted by a lily's scent cannot fail to miss the pollen-bearing anthers.*

WE NORMALLY LEARN TO ASSOCIATE SMELL *with an event or feeling. This means that two people will rarely react to any scent in the same way and that our perception of what defines a smell is an abstract interior map composed of private histories.*

We know very little about the process of smelling save that it does not work like the other senses. As the scent molecules go up our nose the messages go straight to the part of the brain used for feelings and emotions. It hardly ever occurs to us to analyze smells, and if we try, it is incredibly difficult to use language to describe them. We use words like "fruity," "burnt," or "clean" that describe our response to the smell rather than the sensation itself.

It is enough to recognize them, although no one knows how we create a memory bank of fragrances. There is no classification of scent other than the range from pleasant to unpleasant. This may be an evolutionary development designed as a form of protection and attraction, but it means that description of any smell is restricted to analogous sensations. The truth is we dramatically under-use our ability to smell. We have come to confine its use to flavor, the attempt to attract others, and the perception of unpleasant smells. But language betrays its wider purposes: we "smell" danger, "smell" trouble, "smell" the air—these are not just metaphors; they are practical, descriptive phrases. Much of what we call sixth sense is actually smell: we can smell each other, we can smell walls and trees, we can smell the earth.

The closeness of taste and scent cannot be over-stressed. The difference between flavor and fragrance is largely semantic and just as we inevitably have our tastebuds aroused by the smell of food, so it follows that a scent will be "consumed" by us as much as smelled. It feeds and satisfies us in many ways. One of the ironies of this is that there is much overlap between chemical fragrances used for perfumes and food flavorings.

Most natural fragrances are plant-derived. They come either from the volatile, aromatic vegetable oils known as essential oils, or from the non-volatile oils called resins. Lavender is an essential oil and pine produces a powerfully aromatic resin. We are all familiar with plants that smell good—honeysuckle, jasmine, roses, herbs, night-scented stock, tobacco plants on a summer's night, the green tang of grass after the first cut of the year: all these are objectively measurable experiences. We know instantly what someone is talking about when they refer to any of them. But the garden is a mixture of a thousand scents, not just the seasonal list of sweet-smelling plants. There is the smell of dry soil after rain, the smoky tang of a bonfire, and the richness of a handful of soil in early spring; the wet scent of the wind as it flaps around the full greenness of the garden, and the dry whiff of frost. The bitter smell of dock is felt almost as a taste. Stones smell, and gravel releases its own bony scent as it is raked.

All this is part of the sensuous vocabulary of the gardener. All this is to be celebrated as gardening—namely, the rich enjoyment of all the senses, rather than just the mechanical observation of horticultural techniques.

SPRING

Spring is not just a bracketed period on the calendar. The light spreads as the sun climbs a little higher daily, colors lose their winter drab, and the garden creeps out from hiding wearing gorgeous clothes. It is the most exciting moment in any gardener's year. While this excitement is primarily prompted by the visual display unfolding by the day, there are also scents coming into the garden like dear friends walking through the door. The best are all familiar and the powerful trigger that smell has upon memory is most evident in spring.

The most evocative of them all is the smell of newly mown grass. Nothing else in the entire gardening calendar has such an impact as that first green sweetness in the nostril. Scent is always personal, but for me all the pleasures of childhood summer days come flooding back with the first whiff. Cutting grass in midwinter cannot trick this response. To work, it needs sufficient sunshine and sustained warmth for the grass to be growing. This first heat of the year releases all kinds of scents that have been locked in by winter cold or snow. You search for the source of scents that have been waylaid throughout the winter, catching tantalizing whiffs like brief snatches of a distant refrain.

Spring rain is usually more showery than at any other time of year and is sometimes interspersed with puzzlingly contradictory bursts of sunshine—often both occurring simultaneously! This racing, fitful weather has its own smell carried on the wind, lighter and fresher than the rain of other seasons.

Of course the spring flowers are wonderfully scented. From the first snowdrops to the late-season bluebells, bulbs dominate floral scents in the spring garden. Bulbs are like mines lying underground, waiting to explode into glory at the trigger of heat, moisture, or light according to their season. Everything is packaged inside their dry, reclusive shells—leaves, flowers, and, for many, intense scents. In fact bulbs are like a manifestation of scent itself, hidden below the ground of consciousness but reappearing with a startling mix of sensuous recollection.

But not all spring bulbs are particularly fragrant and many that do smell do so only on close inspection. The common snowdrop (*Galanthus nivalis*), for example, is only lightly scented, although the variety 'G. S. Arnott' is strongly fragrant and an excellent, large flower. Most daffodils smell a little but the jonquil (*Narcissus jonquilla*), in its many varieties, is the best to grow for scent—and, for my money, as pretty as any. The early-flowering *Crocus laevigatus* and the rather later *C. chrysanthus* are both sweetly fragrant, which makes them an exception to the rule of rather modestly scented spring crocuses.

Hyacinths smell powerfully, of course, although personally I cannot abide the scent and dislike the flower. *Iris reticulata*, however, I love. It is one of my favorite spring flowers, smelling of violets and looking wonderful with its yellow markings within the richly blue petals.

Most tulips are without scent but the yellow *Tulipa sylvestris* does have a distinct fragrance and is less formally soldierlike than the majority of species, adapting well to naturalization in grass, increasing unaided by underground stolons.

I was brought up in an area of chalky woodland where bluebells (*Hyacinthoides non-scripta*) grow by the million. In consequence I rejoice each spring as I catch the first scent of

I rejoice each spring as I catch the first scent of bluebells.

them and have, unwisely, planted them in my own garden, even though I know that eventually they will become a weed. But better weeds like that than many a deliberate plant!

None of the spring bulbs can match the lilies for fragrance. They have all the richness and intensity of jasmine without the overpowering heaviness. Planting lilies should be done in the same spirit as buying perfume—it is a gift to yourself of pure sensual pleasure from which everyone else will benefit.

OPPOSITE: *Wild daffodils (*Narcissus jonquilla)
*have a very sweet scent that is much more powerful
than most of the more robust daffodil hybrids.*
ABOVE: *The scent of millions of flowers in a
bluebell wood in spring is unmistakable, although it
somehow remains subtle as well as strong.*

Spring is bursting with smelly shrubs. *Ceanothus* x *delileanus* 'Gloire de Versailles', elaeagnus, lilac (*Syringa*), mock orange (*Philadelphus*), the Ghent group of deciduous azaleas, *Viburnum carlesii*, all the daphnes, *Buddleia davidii* and *B. globosa*, *Hamamelis mollis*, magnolia, ribes—the list is long and could be longer. The first rose, *Rosa primula*, has—atypically for a rose—a scent that is owned by spring.

I would make a special plea for the evergreen shrubs that smell sweetly as their flowers tend to be less heralded than the sprint from bare branch to glory that is the way of deciduous shrubs. *Mahonia japonica*, *Choisya ternata*, *Osmanthus delavayii*, *O. fragrans* and *O.* x *burkwoodii*, *Daphne odora*, *Rhododendron fortunei*, *Skimmia japonica,* and *Viburnum* x *burkwoodii* 'Conoy' all have scented flowers that can hold their own in any perfumed deciduous company.

Of all the different types of plant that you can grow in a garden, climbers are the group that contain most promise of scent. This is not least because their flowers are nearer to the nose than a delicate rock plant or bulb. In an age of small back gardens they are efficient with space, offering color, form, and fragrance from a tiny patch of soil with a wall or fence on which to clamber. Although there is a wider choice for a sunny sheltered site, it is possible to find a sweet-smelling climber for virtually any part of any garden. The following are just a few fragrant highlights.

Clematis armandii, with its white, almond-scented flowers and evergreen leaves is a favorite of mine. It likes a sunny, sheltered spot. *C. forsteri* is a lesser known plant, also evergreen, but lemon-scented. *C. montana* 'Odorata' is much more vigorous than either of the previous two and, although it can be pruned back after flowering, it is not for the smallest garden. Like all montanas, its scent is reminiscent of vanilla.

Another very vigorous climber is *Lonicera japonica* 'Halliana'; it is usually the first honeysuckle into flower and, like all honeysuckles, it smells wonderful, especially in the evening. Plant it against a wall that catches the evening light so that you

But it is not just bulbs that scent the air at this time of year. The delicate spring fragrance of *Primula vulgaris*, the wild primrose, gives me as much pleasure as the most voluptuous scent of a lily in high summer; the unsubtle, almost crude scent of wallflowers (*Erysimum*) and Brompton stocks (*Matthiola incana*) is an essential component of spring for me. Scented-leaved pelargoniums will release their perfume when squeezed from mid-spring onward; they include *P. tomentosum*, which has a strong peppermint aroma, and *P. capitatum*, which smells of roses.

will be drawn to sit close to it in the evening light, thus making the most of its fruity sweetness.

The first flowers of *Jasminum* x *stephanense* will come out in late spring and last throughout the summer. Unlike honeysuckle, jasmine can be overpowering so it needs planting away from a seat or door so that the rich scent is carried sweetly across the air rather than suffocating you.

Wisteria falls into that mid-season of late spring/early summer that depends so much on the vagaries of the weather. But whenever the long racemes of flowers bloom they always smell superb with a honey pea-like fragrance. *W. sinensis* flowers before the leaves develop and is a better choice for scent than *W. floribunda*; the white form (*W. sinensis* 'Alba') is more exquisitely scented than the much more common violet variety.

However, there are a few spring smells that are distinctive of the season which I dislike: the flowering currant (*Ribes sanguineum*) has a smell (or rather stench—definitely not a scent) that is repulsive. It astonishes me that it is still freely planted. The appropriately named bog plant skunk cabbage (*Lysichiton americanus*) has bananalike spathes growing out of seemingly barren mud that are sufficiently wonderful to force one to put up with their unmistakable smell. Mercifully these are the exceptions that prove the rule. Of all the seasons, none is so entrancingly fragrant as spring.

OPPOSITE: *The most evocative scent of all is from the first cut of grass in spring, returning to us with a pang of excitement.*
TOP RIGHT: *Wallflowers (*Erysimum cheiri*) are biennials with a warm musty fragrance that for me is one of the defining scents of spring.*
BOTTOM RIGHT: *The wild primrose (*Primula vulgaris*) is a woodland flower whose preciously delicate fragrance is the true harbinger of spring. An absolute joy.*

SUMMER

One of the happier antitheses of summer is that many of its best treasures only fully reveal themselves at night, when the essences of summer—light and heat—have begun to fade. Flowers that release their scent at night do so to attract moths and other night-flying insects. They tend to be white or pale-colored, which obviously increases their visibility, and they release their scent as the air cools. This reduces the competition to find a pollinator as well as increasing the chances of the pollinating insect moving onto another plant from the same family, both devices designed to improve evolutionary success.

The best of all these nighttime performers is the tobacco plant (*Nicotiana sylvestris*), which at dusk gives off the most delicious and evocative of all garden scents: rich, musky, and utterly sensual. Others might include night-scented stock (*Matthiola bicornis*), honeysuckles (*Lonicera*), night-blooming jasmine (*Cestrum nocturnum*), *Hoya carnosa*, datura, the evening primrose (*Oenothera biennis*), and all the white-flowering shrubs, such as philadelphus, syringa, and osmanthus.

Roses loom out of a miasma of summer scent and color as soon as one considers shrubs as part of the armory of garden aromas. In fact this influence is disproportionately large, because the best shrub roses dominate the garden for a period of no more than a few weeks. There is no space here to celebrate the virtues of individual roses, but I would urge you to explore the virtues of the albas, which are all delicately but thrillingly fragrant; all as tough as brambles; all bearing wonderful flowers; and most clothed with especially lovely foliage.

My favorite place to sit in summer is in our herb garden, which is a mixture of herbs and old roses. Each year, for about a month in early summer, the roses are the stars of the garden, outstandingly lovely to look at and all laden with their own

idiosyncratic perfume. Rose scent rarely wafts on the air; you have to nuzzle up to them and smell their fragrance as you might savor the bouquet of a fine wine. I grow centifolias, damasks, albas, gallicas, bourbons, hybrid perpetuals, moss roses, and rugosas with the herbs. All have superb scents.

During this brief four- or five-week period the herbs play second fiddle, but after the decline of the roses the scents of lavender, rosemary, thyme, mint, sweet woodruff, borage, hyssop, bay, and dozens of other herbs all shade the air, especially when they are brushed past or fingered. In every garden I have made I have tried to incorporate a sheltered herb garden that is also the main outdoor eating area, to make the most of these delicious fragrances.

Of course a midsummer's day is filled with an almost bewildering variety of scent from the perfumed subtlety of alba or centifolia roses to the knock'em out blast of lilies and the

musky sharpness of pelargoniums or box leaves. But the one smell that is more heart-racingly beautiful than the scent of any plant, and impossible to capture or contain within a garden, is the smell of warm, dusty soil immediately after a light shower of rain. The water releases an aroma of such fecundity that you almost expect growth to start erupting around you like time-lapse photography. There are usually just a couple of such moments each summer and every time I am freshly startled by the power of their loveliness.

Old shrub roses have all the best smells. Here are a few plucked at random from dozens of alternatives (from left to right): Rosa *'Boule de Neige',* R. *'New Dawn',* R. *'Constance Spry', and* R. gallica *'Charles de Mills'.*

Every garden deserves to have at least one climbing rose and the more restricted the space, the more the need for it to smell as well as look good. If you have only shade, *Rosa* 'Souvenir du Docteur Jamain' will grow quite happily in it, producing its dark velvet flowers well into the autumn and smelling—astonishingly —of apricots. If you have a sunny wall, you are spoiled for rosy choice. *R.* 'New Dawn' is both easy and lovely; *R.* 'Madame Alfred Carrière' is even more obliging and is also strongly scented. *R.* 'Madame Plantier' is more often grown as a bush than as a climbing rose, which is a pity as it will train well against a fence and it has the alba's exquisite fragrance.

Annuals have to do it all in a season, growing, flowering, attracting pollinators, and dying in the time that it takes for an herbaceous plant to settle into its planting site. This makes them especially brightly colored and, where color alone will not suffice, especially strongly scented. Biennials have another whole season but, along with annuals, they are still the sprinters of the garden.

If you are not in the swing of gardening, it can be rather like watching dancers execute a square dance from the edge of the floor: it seems a complicated procedure that is evidently giving the participants enormous pleasure and which they perform with the greatest of ease. Their satisfaction serves only to highlight one's own incompetence. Growing annuals can seem a similarly daunting task, whereas in reality it is simply a case of tossing some seeds onto a piece of raked ground—they will do everything else for you. This technique can be refined a little via the use of seed trays and the process of thinning out seedlings, but in essence that is all there is to it. Having grasped this principle, you can fill gaps quickly or even create entire borders in your garden within a matter of weeks, following fancy rather than a gardening manual. If it doesn't work, it has only cost a few packs of seed and much experience has been gained.

Not all annuals and biennials are worth planting for smell alone, but I shall mention a few that seem to me to be essential. I make no apologies for taking yet another opportunity to sing the praises of the flowering tobacco (*Nicotiana*

sylvestris), an annual with the most muskily exotic scent of all. Wallflowers (*Erysimum*) also have an instantly recognizable spicy aroma and will, as their name suggests, grow out of a solid wall. I know of a castle in Wales where they flower 50 ft. (15 m) up on the side of a twelfth-century tower. Despite being perennials, they should be treated as biennials.

I love annuals that grow in a clever jumble, mixing colors and scents in an instinctive and chance manner, much in the spirit of traditional English cottage gardens. The pot-marigold (*Calendula officinalis*) is a hardy annual that works well in this manner, with a sharp, tangy scent. Happily my herb garden is infested with sweet rocket (*Hesperis matronalis*),

OPPOSITE: *Cistus in the foreground combines with climbing and shrub roses. It makes good sense to focus sweetly scented planting around doors and windows, using the reflective heat of a wall to encourage the fragrance.*

ABOVE: Nicotiana sylvestris *is my favorite scent of high summer, enriching the night air with its musky perfume.*

another perennial that behaves like a biennial, and which I encourage simply by not deterring it and allowing it to sow seed year after year. Its big white and violet flowers delicately taint the evening air with fragrance.

Another flower that flags its fragrance in its name is the sweet pea (*Lathyrus odoratus*), an annual that is best sown in autumn or in early spring. It has a delicious vanilla scent. I like the way that annuals have accumulated folk names, personalizing them and driving away the frightening specter of Latin and the huge body of one's own ignorance. Who could fail to love any flower called the poached-egg plant (*Limnanthes douglasii*) or sweet William (*Dianthus barbatus*), Virginia stock (*Malcolmia maritima*), candytuft (*Iberis amara*), night-scented stock (*Matthiola bicornis*), or snapdragon (*Antirrhinum majus*)? All add much to the scented garden, all are easy to grow, and all have real character.

Cosmos atrosanguineus is a tuber with a decisively chocolatey smell—which makes it a good plant; it is also a lovely dark crimson (usually described as chocolate in color, but it isn't)—which makes it a very good plant indeed. Dahlias, tubers again, have no significant smell. Neither do most of the gladioli, which are corms, but *Gladiolus callianthus* does, and its white, dark-centered flowers are a good late-summer addition to the scented garden.

Summer scents are dominated by the honeysuckles, mainly because most are so easy to grow. *Lonicera periclymenum* is the common honeysuckle of the hedgerow and it is normally sold under the guise of its two best-known varieties 'Belgica' and 'Serotina'. Both of these have yellow flowers that are splashed with purple and both suffuse the evening air with a heady fragrance. *L. × americana* is reputed to smell strongly of cloves; it is certainly strongly fragrant, although cloves are not the scented yardstick that I would reach for.

It is a lovely climber nevertheless. *L. caprifolium* possesses the instantly recognizable honeysuckle scent, but creamier flowers than the other species.

The scents of summer do not belong exclusively to flowers. Heat activates the aromatic oils or resins present in the foliage of many plants so they will smell strongest at this time of year. It is your hands that carry the scent of most leaves to your nose. That or your feet and body, crushing and pushing past leaves that need bruising to release their fragrance.

that they can spill across your way and you can snatch their scent from your brusque passing.

The leaves of all the rockroses (*Cistus* and *Helianthemum*) emit a pungent, resinous aroma, especially on hot days. You can see the waxy gum that produces this smell, glistening on the leaves in the heat. The maquis of Corsica and Sardinia has miles of it, stickily catching against you as you push through it. The gum is called labdanum and is particularly abundant after a cool night following a hot day. It is collected and used against bronchitis. *Cistus ladanifer* is especially productive of labdanum.

A gentler scent and one needing no bruising contact is the fragrance of apples that comes from the foliage of the species rose *Rosa eglanteria*, the sweet briar. There is a lightness and freshness about this that lifts the heart in early summer when, after a sudden shower, the washed air is touched with the delicious fragrance from the young leaves. The incense rose (*Rosa primula*) has incense-scented delicate leaves that, like the sweet briar, will smell especially clear after rain.

All these plants respond to heat and on a warm, still summer's day they will need no contact to fill the air with their wonderful scent.

Of course there are plants like the scented-leafed pelargoniums that specialize in this, making it their prime piece of theater and producing astonishingly vivid aromas, but in fact almost every kind of leaf will smell of something if rolled in the fingers and gently sniffed. It is just that our language and analytical faculties become heavy and cumbersome when attempting to describe smells, so we usually resort to conveying the quantity of scent rather than the quality.

In this light, it is not surprising that we tend to focus on those leaves that smell a lot. The best known, and in some cases the best, tend to be herbs. In addition to those I have already mentioned from my own garden, the rich oils of basil, sage, lemon-verbena (*Aloysia triphylla*), peppermint, marjoram, oregano, curry plant (*Helichrysum italicum*), bay, *Artemisia* 'Powis Castle', and santolina are all released when they are crushed. For this reason the woodier, shrubby plants are best planted at the edge of paths, so

Cosmos astrosanguineus has a distinctly chocolate smell that is almost as rich as its burgundy color.

AUTUMN

Of all the seasons autumn is the one that you first sense with your nose. There is a feeling of time passing in the air, a whiff of mortality that makes the last beautiful days of the gardening year all the more poignantly beautiful.

The garden falls into the year's dotage (how much more apt is the American "fall" for this season!) and as it does so the sugars in foliage, fruits, and seeds concentrate, making the moment of ripeness also the moment of irreversible decay. It is this mixture of harvest and regret, fulfillment and loss that makes autumn the most equivocal of seasons, the scents all combining to bring pleasure tinged with sorrow at their passing.

Like spring, autumn is not all of a piece. The first half is often summer-hot and dry, with only the shortening of the days and the searing of the leaves to betray the season. The second half falls hard into winter, so that in the north a frosty day in November bears no seasonal resemblance to a warm September afternoon. The scents vary likewise. Early autumn mornings are heavy with dew, lifting into days that are often as hot as any in the year. This means that the fruitiness that is so characteristic of this season reaches the nostrils with a moist tang intensified by heat. There is a hint of the fading away of flower and leaf and yet it is wrong to measure early fall as a decline; in many ways this is the absolute peak of the year and the scents that mark it are rich and at their zenith—from perfect pears and tomatoes to the final flourish of repeat-flowering roses and the summer flowers and tender herbs that keep performing until the first frosts.

The large-flowering clematis are undistinguished by scent, but in autumn the late-flowering come into their own. *C. rehderiana* and *C. flammula* are both superbly scented as well as very beautiful. *Jasminum officinale* can usually be trusted to enrich the air well into the first frosts and *Lonicera periclymenum* 'Graham Thomas' has an exceptionally long—and well-scented—season.

The range of autumn-flowering scented shrubs is limited, but makes a select band. *Buddleia auriculata* is tender, but is worth risking for its highly fragrant creamy spikes if you have a warm, sheltered site. The autumn witch hazel (*Hamamelis virginiana*) is delicately scented and *Clerodendrum trichotomum* has leaves that are typically musty but flowers that are intensely scented.

Then mid-autumn tilts the balance. We associate decay with something that is inherently repulsive, but in the garden it can be a very sensuous and pleasurable experience. As rotting vegetation dissolves into itself the scent that it makes is, in its own way, as seductive as ground coffee or the richness of a good cigar. It is not alluring or sharp but wonderfully soft and mature.

So much of autumn is bound to the death of deciduous leaves. Their coloration and then fall, the truffly smell of their wetness in drifts on the ground, and their final disintegration are all held as much in the nose as in the eye.

The scent of a bonfire is slow and pervasive and richly evocative, lingering in the fading autumnal light. Note, however, that most states and localities in the U.S.A. require permits for open burning.

There is a feeling of time passing in the air, a whiff of mortality that makes the last beautiful days of the gardening year all the more poignantly beautiful.

When I was a child the beech leaves fell in drifts across the lawn and would be swept up with a besom—the old-fashioned witch's broom of a child's story—gathered with wooden "boards"—simply fashioned planks of wood nailed together that had been used only for that purpose for decades—and taken to a special heap for leaves. Over the years this became leaf mold, a rich, black, crumbly compost that smelled both clean and decayed, bringing back in the spring all the fading glamor of the autumnal days when the leaves were collected.

Although it is now considered ecologically incorrect, and in some countries actually illegal, autumn is also the season of bonfires, of heaps of slow-burning leaves and weeds, the sticks and twigs collected in the general sweeping. The smell of smoke hangs over the thin afternoon air like a comforting old jacket, and clings to the real jacket, and hair, for hours afterward, bringing the past and the vastness of sky and fire into the sanitized safety of the home.

Finally the last weeks of autumn bring frost to many areas, and with it the clean-smelling bone hardness that is first known with the nose. Stand in the garden on a chilly autumnal night when a frost is forecast and smell the air. The ice is there in your nostrils like a figure in the corner of your eye. Memory, if not the conscious mind, will instantly know that winter is coming.

OPPOSITE: *Each season is known by its smells as much as anything else and it is not just flowers that smell. Autumn brings its own rich mix of scents from sodden leaves, the soil—wet but still warm—and the gentle decay of plants.*
RIGHT *The days of dry leaves lying thick on the ground are few (top) and they have their own crisp scent that is quite different from the more familiar smell of wet leaves. The scents of ripeness balance on a knife-edge of decay (bottom), which is the essence of autumnal melancholy.*

WINTER

There is a tendency to close the garden down in winter—mentally, physically, and sensuously. This is a pity, especially in the northern hemisphere, where the winter months can amount to a third of the year or more. Grass is at the heart of this problem. Most people in the north base their garden around lawns and grass paths, which are wonderful in spring and summer but become unattractive and often unpleasantly muddy or covered with snow throughout winter. If you have "hard" paths and small paved or graveled areas, then the garden remains accessible for the whole year.

In mild, snowless regions the whole gardening cycle begins in winter with the care and preparation of the earth so that it will feed plants the following year. One of the things that I enjoy most about digging (and there are lots of things I enjoy about it) is the smell of the earth that is released by the spade cutting in and lifting clods that have been buried for a year. Not only does the soil itself have real scent, but the roots of the crop or plant—even weed—that has been growing there will also contribute to the mix, creating something new out of the vague remnants of last season's garden.

The crisp tang of a frosty morning almost leaps out of the page from this wonderful winter photograph of Jacques Wirtz's nursery garden in Belgium.

I have two conflicting attitudes for making the most of winter scents. The first is strategically to position sweet-smelling shrubs and climbers a short distance from the house so that you are enticed out into the garden to enjoy them, and the second is to group all the winter-flowering and winter-scented plants near to the back door so that they can be enjoyed with as little trouble as possible. The upshot of this dilemma is that I do both.

The thing to bear in mind is that you are unlikely to sit for long in the winter garden, so scents should not be focused around seats as they might be for the rest of the year. It is enough to approach, stop, sniff, be enchanted, and move on. Organize little groups of sweetly scented plants like posies during the winter months. Although the range of smelly plants is small, it encompasses a rich variety and can provide scent as sweet as any summer border.

Snowdrops (*Galanthus nivalis*) are truly winter flowers and deliciously scented, if somewhat retentively so. Flower and nose have to meet if you are to know the scent properly.

The one clematis that will flower in winter in all areas, providing it has a warm, sheltered wall behind it, is *C. cirrhosa balearica*. It smells so good and looks so comfortable once established that it scarcely needs accompaniment. The scent from its speckled interior is elusively lemon and, like so many clematis, a spray of it makes a wonderful cut flower, the fragrance intensifying within the confines of a room. The winter-flowering honeysuckle (*Lonicera fragrantissima*) has delicate little white flowers on bare stems that will also haunt a room for days with their fragrance if placed in a jar.

In many ways shrubs are the ideal plants for modern life. They need little care once planted, provide shape and structure, leaf and flower, and often wonderful scent. Winter-flowering shrubs nearly all have good scent, doubling their already high value. *Viburnum* x *bodnantense* is a reliable winter standby for scented flowers, which appear on bare stems. *V.* x *b.* 'Dawn' has large globes of pink flowers and *V.* x *b.* 'Deben' white flowers opening from pink buds, both smelling increasingly intense as winter wears on. *V. farreri* is another essential for the winter garden and will flower intermittently all winter long, always carrying its almond and honey fragrance.

Wintersweet (*Chimonanthus praecox*) takes as long as five years to flower, but it is worth the wait, producing golden bells on its bare stems with a delicious honey scent. It is best against a sunny wall, protected from cold winds. Another yellow flower produced on leafless branches is the witch hazel (*Hamamelis mollis*); the flowers are like saffron spiders. *H. vernalis* has an even stronger scent and the flowers are a deep, almost orange yellow.

Evergreen plants that flower in winter and smell good are earning their keep three times over. The Christmas box (*Sarcococca*) is one such plant, mahonia another. I once lived in a house with a long drive that had, slightly alarmingly, a double row of redwoods interplanted with *Mahonia japonica,* and throughout late winter and early spring the gloomy driveway was suffused with the mahonia's delicious honey scent.

Unfortunately, not all fragrant winter-flowering plants can bloom or even survive in cold regions. *Daphne mezereum* is a tough little shrub known as February daphne, but it often skips February altogether, saving its powerful scent for spring. I had one by the back door of our house in town and for a few weeks each year around St. Valentine's Day its clove-sweet fragrance was the first thing to greet me in the morning. Most smells trigger our powers of remembrance, but that daphne always fires me with a promise of spring, however wintry the weather.

RIGHT: *Many of the scented winter- to- early-spring flowers are produced on bare stems, before their leaves emerge, so all attention is focused on them. Four of the best are (clockwise from top left): winter-flowering honeysuckle (*Lonicera fragrantissima*); wintersweet (*Chimonanthus praecox); flowering quince (*Chaenomeles speciosa 'Nivalis'); witch hazel (*Hamamelis x intermedia 'Diane').*

TREES

Because they catch every wind, trees can spread their fragrance farthest across—and by the same token beyond—the garden. It follows that the most scented trees should be planted upwind of the prevailing airflow. By virtue of their size and the way that they trap smells within the confines of their branches, aromatic trees are an important part of the sensuous garden and there is a significant range to choose from.

Scent in a tree can come from a number of sources: flowers, foliage, fruit, or resin, and occasionally a combination of these. But more often there will be one dominant aspect that fixes its scent in our mind.

Trees tend to flower in a brief flurry of scent and color in spring and then subside into their more sober everyday wear of foliage, but while this short floral display lasts they can be very impressive indeed. As I write in early June, the countryside outside my window is gloriously wreathed in hawthorn (*Crataegus monogyna*) and elder (*Sambucus nigra*) bloom; the scent of the former is strong to the point of rankness and the latter fruitily sophisticated. A month ago the orchards were rich with the delicate fragrance of apple blossoms, and before that with the stronger-scented crab apples that I have planted around my garden boundary.

In a nearby garden a huge horse chestnut (*Aesculus hippocastanum*) has just finished flowering and the unusual easterly winds we had this spring wafted its scent through our opened windows. It was not until I was standing beneath the tree, talking to its owner, that I realized that this was what I had been smelling for the previous few days.

Another common British tree, the lime, has many garden forms, all of which have heavily scented flowers. Avoid *Tilia platyphyllos* because it drips honeydew from its inevitable aphid infestation, and *T. tomentosa* and its forms because the flowers are toxic but irresistible to bees. *T. cordata*, the small-leafed lime, is perhaps the best garden choice for scent.

Most magnolias are large shrubs, but a few make genuine trees. In warm areas *Magnolia grandiflora* can become a superb evergreen tree reaching 90 ft. (27 m); in harsher climates it is better as a wall-trained shrub. However grown, it will produce highly scented creamy-white flowers—although it may take up

to twenty years to do so. The lily tree (*M. heptapeta*) is a deciduous tree with fragrant, pure white, cup-shaped flowers. The leaves of the big-leaf magnolia (*M. macrophylla*), from the south-eastern states, are enormous; the flowers are equally gargantuan and powerfully scented.

Laburnums have become part of a gardening cliché; the laburnum tunnel, as overpowering to the nose as to the eye. But do not despise them for this. Planted simply, their sprays of yellow flowers breathe their perfume into open air where it disperses before becoming overwhelming. The Scotch laburnum (*L. alpinum*) is a better bet than the common *L. anagyroides*.

Early in the year the buds of the balsam poplar (*Populus balsamifera*) are sticky with balsam and are strongly aromatic, heralding their imminent burst into leaf and the advent of spring with drenching waves of sweet scent.

There are over four hundred species of eucalyptus trees that will grow in temperate gardens; all have leaves filled with a fragrant oil, giving them a wide range of scent from the peppermint smell of *E. coccifera*, the Tasmanian snow gum, to the rather more tender, lemon-scented gum (*E. citriodora*).

The leaves of the western red cedar (*Thuja plicata*) smell lovely when crushed, giving off a strong whiff of pear drops. *T. standishii* smells of lemon. Junipers smell resinous and if you are on acid soil the Oregon Douglas fir (*Pseudotsuga menziesii*) is equally pleasant in its pungency. Most pines smell definitively of themselves and in the right place that makes them superb garden trees. The fruity smell of the walnut tree (*Juglans regia*) has to be shaken out by the wind. Like many garden scents, it is one that we catch only intermittently, when conditions are right, but it is the rarity of such scents that makes them all the more precious.

FROM LEFT TO RIGHT: *Horse chestnut* (Aesculus hippocastanum) *is perhaps the most magnificent of all flowering trees; the flowers of linden (*Tilia) *are less obvious but their scent is powerful enough to fill the air and is attractive to bees. The scent of some trees comes from their resin. None are more distinctive than the eucalyptus, and the pines, like this Montezuma pine.*

INTUITION

Gardens are a statement about

ourselves, and if your garden makes

you, the gardener, feel good, then it is

certain that it will look good.

ABOVE: *You do not need to know anything about a plant to know that it is beautiful.*

Here the new shoots of a spruce emerge as an abstract picture of loveliness.

FEELING

The essence of sensuous gardening is to allow yourself to be intimate with your garden. Consider it as private as your bedroom. Garden just for yourself and your own needs. I once read an article about women working in business who felt they had to obey a formal dress code to meet the expectations of men. They tolerated this because beneath this outer layer they could wear the underwear that pleased them and that was often as sensuous and luxurious as their outer clothing was drab and conventional. Gardens should be like this. They are the underwear you choose to please yourself, not the formal attire imposed by other people's expectations.

It is tempting to judge a garden as a finite thing—like a sculpture, film, or painting. This is inappropriate. Any garden changes by the hour, let alone from season to season and year to year. The only way to know it at all is to experience it in all weathers, to forgo any attempts to possess it, and, ideally, to become part of it. Everything changes all the time, including our own perceptions and sensations. There are no external yardsticks to measure how we feel about stimuli. Have faith in your own responses and garden for your own private pleasure. In doing so you will surely give and share that pleasure with more people than if you garden by the book. A flower that we may casually admire in passing one day

will reduce us to tears of joy the next. It is not the plants that do this to us: it is we who react and respond to them.

Gardens are about people. Every garden tells you as much about the people that made it and live in it as about the plants that compose it. If we recognize that making a garden is an expression of ourselves and a statement about us, then we might take the business of experiencing it fully more seriously. But as yet gardeners—especially expert

We are programed into seeking conventional images of beauty from a garden rather than trusting our own responses. A garden does not have to be tightly controlled to be beautiful.

The choices we make relating to most areas of our lives are based on a blend of experience, observation, and knowledge, and a bad or wrong decision, perhaps about a dish in a restaurant or a particular article of clothing bought on a whim, is used to enable us to make a more informed choice next time. However, we feel that there is a set of rules, a list of names, and an almost masonic series of rituals to be observed before we can begin to enjoy our own garden. This is sad because it is so clearly false.

During a recent lunch at the Chelsea Flower Show in London my companions at the table were all experienced and well-known garden writers. There was unanimous agreement that none of us practiced what we preached. It was a case of "Do as I say, not as I do." Why then, I asked, do they bother to preach it at all? Why not be truthful? But the consensus was that only the experienced and knowledgeable could risk breaking the rules with impunity.

But there are no rules. Or at least, the rules that do exist are merely guidelines, there to be broken freely by everyone. Plants can be planted at any time, pruned at any time, and enjoyed all the time.

ones—have a tendency to scoff at this. They feel happier dealing with the practical realities of technique than with what they see as the impractical mumbo-jumbo of feelings. More fool them. They are missing out on the best half of it.

There are no rules

People who daily exercise great choice over food, clothing, interior design, cars, music, and entertainment, otherwise sophisticated people, become inarticulate novices when it comes to gardening.

We all do things as and when we can or want to in the garden. Of course there are times to do things that are better than others, and the rhythm of the seasons cannot be ignored, but in all but the very short term it hardly makes any difference at all. Plants are remarkably tough and will recover within a year from anything but the cruelest of treatment. Here is my list of non-rules, based upon years of fielding gardening questions:

Planting

Learn to love the actual business of planting. The better the ground is prepared, the more the plant will thrive. Always dig big holes and always enrich with compost. There are absolutely no short cuts to this, so enjoy the process itself. I consider planting to be the most sensuous, exciting activity in the garden. The best analogy is to cooking: making the dish is as creative and stimulating as eating it.

Anything can be planted or moved at any time, but consider the move to be like a piece of surgery. However healthy, the patient will need time to recover and if the operation is major, a period of intensive care. Always water thoroughly after planting, even if it coincides with heavy rain. The fitter and healthier the plant is before moving (be it from one site to another or from a container into the ground), the better its chances of survival. The smaller and more dormant the plant, the better its chances, too.

Pruning

If in doubt, you can do no harm by pruning immediately after flowering. Remember: no plant needs pruning; we prune for human, not horticultural, requirements. On balance, however, the best time to prune is when you have the right tool in your hand and are prepared to do the job.

Grass

Relax. Grass is very, very tough. To get the best out of it you need plenty of water, good drainage, and rich soil. Cut it only once a week and enjoy its greenness rather than its neatness. Moss looks nice and is a symptom of poor drainage and shade rather than being a problem in its own right.

Weeds

Little and often is the secret. Never let them get on top of you. However, if they do, try to cut them back before they seed. Weed seeds are the real enemy, not weeds themselves. It is far better to cut a weedy patch with a mower until such a time as you can weed it than to slowly hand weed it over the summer.

Watering

Better to water heavily once a week than lightly every day. Water deeply so that it reaches right down to the roots rather than just the top inch of soil. Mulch to stop evaporation. Water before plants show signs of drought, not in response to it.

In the end you must trust your intuition. Your intuition will tell you what feels right, without the need for a manual to explain why. Intuition works directly off your own sensations before you have a chance to butt in and analyze them. Trust your own hunches and sensations. Only you know what sounds evoke pleasure in you, what looks good to your eye, tastes good in your mouth, feels good to your hand, or what scents you like. Throw away the gardening manuals and trust yourself. Gardening is about private feeling and enjoyment, and nobody knows these things better than you. There is no examiner, no moral worth cast over your horticultural efforts. Gardening is like sex: if everyone involved is happy, then you are doing it right.

A tiara of dew caught in the strands of a cobweb (left top) is as lovely and just as much a part of our experience of gardening as anything we could grow. Sometimes accidents are so much better than careful design (top right). Bindweed (below left) is a terrible problem and has to be eradicated, but here, growing through a yew hedge, it is just terribly beautiful. No diamond ever had a more exquisite setting (below right) than this drop of rain in the leaves of a lupine.

PLANT DIRECTORY

The following is a selection of my favorite plants from each chapter. Obviously the choice is idiosyncratic and you may find there are glaring omissions. But that is what sensuous gardening is all about—choosing plants you like for your own personal reasons.

The sizes given are those of a mature plant growing in an ideal situation; adverse soil and light conditions will dramatically stunt an otherwise healthy plant. The first figure refers to height; the second to width.

Numbers in bold indicate hardiness zones (see key below). In practice, it is always the precise combination of conditions that affects plants rather than any hard and fast absolutes. In my experience the right soil conditions and sufficient shelter are the most important considerations in a plant's health.

It is assumed that, unless specifically stated to the contrary, everything will be given well-dug, richly manured, weed-free conditions, with exactly the right amount of sun, water, and shelter. And if you achieve that with all your plants you certainly do not need me to tell you how to cultivate them.

Zone 1	Below −50°F
Zone 2	−50° to −40°F
Zone 3	−40° to −30°F
Zone 4	−30° to −20°F
Zone 5	−20° to −10°F
Zone 6	−10° to 0°F
Zone 7	0° to 10°F
Zone 8	10° to 20°F
Zone 9	20° to 30°F

TOUCH

Aesculus hippocastanum
(European horse chestnut) **4–7**
Size: 75 x 50 ft. (23 x 15 m)
Description: One of the largest of deciduous flowering trees with wonderful candelabras of flowers in spring and rich brown seeds or "conkers" in autumn.
Cultivation: Uncommon in the U.S.A., but easy to grow and very long lived.

Betula papyrifera (paper birch) **3–7**
Size: 50 x 25 ft. (15 x 7.5 m)
Description: Makes a large, rather open tree with very distinctive white bark that peels off in great strips.
Cultivation: Very hardy, fast growing, generally unfussy about soil and situation. It will tolerate boggy soil, but will not achieve full height on chalk.

Carex flagillifera **6–8**
Size: 3 x 6 ft. (90 cm x 1.8 m)
Description: This sedge has long, wispy, hair-like strands with gingery leaves.
Cultivation: Prefers sun and rich soil but needs good drainage.

Castanea sativa (sweet chestnut, Spanish chestnut) **6–8**
Size: 100 x 50 ft. (30 x 15 m)
Description: As the tree matures the bark begins to spiral in ridges around the trunk, creating a unique texture. Seeds have a spiky yellow casing in autumn.
Cultivation: Prefers acidic soil. Fast growing to maturity, then very long lived—over 1,000 years. Coppices strongly and is used commercially for poles.

Foeniculum vulgare (fennel) **4–9**
Size: 6 x 2 ft. (1.8m x 60 cm)
Description: Tall herb with very fine, feathery leaves and umbels of yellow flowers. There is also a bronze form.
Cultivation: Fennel grows wild in dry, poor soil but flourishes in well-drained, sunny borders and herb gardens. Although perennial, it is best treated as a biennial. It grows extremely easily from seed.

Gunnera manicata **8–10**
Size: 8 x 10 ft. (2.5 x 3 m)
Description: Herbaceous perennial like giant rhubarb with huge "elephant's ears" leaves that are surprisingly prickly.
Cultivation: Needs moist or even wet conditions and full sun. Crowns must have protection from frost, especially in spring. Ideal for planting on banks of streams or beside ponds.

Pelargonium 'Lady Plymouth'
(scented-leaved geranium) **9–10** **(annual)**
Size: 16 x 18 in. (40 x 45 cm)
Description: Cream-edged leaves with small mauve flowers. When squeezed the leaves release a deliciously musky scent. One of the many examples of two, seemingly unrelated, senses working inextricably together.
Cultivation: Tender perennial that likes sun and well-drained soil. Easy to propagate from cuttings.

Prunus serrula (Tibetan cherry) **5–6**
Size: 20 x 10 ft. (6 x 10 m)
Description: Grown for its shiny auburn bark, peeling in distinctive bands.
Cultivation: Very hardy tree, tolerating most soils and situations, but would prefer to be in full sun.

Sequoiadendron giganteum
(big tree, wellingtonia) **6–9**
Size: up to 300 ft. (90 m)
Description: Huge evergreen tree from the Sierra Nevada of California. Has thick spongy bark.
Cultivation: Only suitable for large gardens. Will tolerate most soils and has adapted remarkably well to introduction in other parts of the world. Best planted in an open position where the full shape can develop.

Stachys byzantina
(lambs' ears) **4–8**
Size: 3 x 1½ ft. (90 x 45 cm)
Description: The whole plant is wooly and soft and the gray leaves produce stems that are topped with rather half-hearted lilac flowers.
Cultivation: Likes full sun and is very happy in dry conditions.

Verbascum olympicum **6–8**
Size: 6 x 2 ft. (1.8m x 60 cm)
Description: Biennial. Tall spires of yellow flowers with velvety felted gray leaves.
Cultivation: Prefers full sun and will tolerate very dry conditions.

Zelkova carpinifolia **6–8**
Size: 80 x 30 ft. (25 x 9 m)
Description: Has been described, in winter, as an "upturned brush." And it does have extraordinary shock of branches growing from the "handle" of the trunk, which develops into fantastic buttresses as it matures.
Cultivation: Shade tolerant, thriving on deep moist soils. Although related to the elms, zelkovas do not suffer from Dutch elm disease.

SIGHT

Structure

Buxus sempervirens (box) **6–8**
Size: up to 15 ft. (4.5 m)
Description: Evergreen with masses of tiny green leaves, with variegated varieties also available. Good for formal hedges that need to be kept clipped low, and for smaller topiary specimens.
Cultivation: Hardy in its zones. Grows in any soil that is not waterlogged and is extremely tolerant of shade. Clip to shape either immediately after last frosts of spring or just before first frosts of autumn. Box will re-grow from drastic cutting back. Roots spread, so chop them back with a spade every few years. Cuttings taken in early autumn will make well-rooted plants a year later.

Carpinus betulus (European hornbeam) **5–8**
Size: up to 60 x 40 ft. (18 x 12 m)
Description: Very similar to beech but with deeper-veined, intense green leaves, turning russet in autumn and not falling until the following spring.
Cultivation: Although it will grow anywhere, hornbeam performs best on heavier soils. As with all hedges it responds enthusiastically to richly cultivated conditions and plenty of water. Will train easily and hold shape well. Clip annually in late summer.

Ilex aquifolium (English holly) **7–9**
Size: up to 80 ft. (25 m)
Description: Evergreen, with shiny, spike-edged leaves and bright red berries produced in winter.

Cultivation: Once established holly will survive very dry, shady conditions, but will flourish best in full sun and rich soil. It hates being moved, so plant as small as possible and then leave alone.

Onopordum acanthium
(Scotch thistle) **biennial**
Size: up to 10 x 3 ft. (3 m x 90 cm)
Description: Silvery gray, downy-leaved plant covered in spiky leaves and prickles.
Cultivation: Biennial, can be sown in autumn or in spring, transplanted to position in late summer or autumn. Self-sows with abandon. Grows best in free-draining soil in full sun. Happy with chalky conditions. Survives drought well.

Taxus baccata (English yew) **6–7**
Size: up to 70 ft. (22 m) (as a tree)
Description: Dark, dense, evergreen foliage is the ideal subject for topiary, and makes the best formal hedge.
Cultivation: Yew grows in full sun or deep shade and any soil that is well drained. Clip in late summer, but it withstands any amount of pruning and training, and will re-grow from the most severe cutting back. Will live thousands of years. Is best propagated from cuttings.

Brown

Helianthus annuus 'Velvet Queen' (sunflower) **annual**
Size: 5 x 1 ft. (1.5 m x 30 cm)
Description: Intensely dark and rich annual flowers on relatively short stems.
Cultivation: Tolerant of most soil conditions, but needs sunshine. Sow directly where it is to flower in spring or start each large seed into growth in an individual pot, and plant out after all danger of frost has passed.

Helleborus orientalis **4–9**
Size: 1½ x 1½ ft. (45 x 45 cm)
Description: Blackish-brown flowers in early spring above evergreen, deeply divided foliage. Rare.
Cultivation: Has deep roots so dig in plenty of organic matter before planting. Needs fertile, moist soil with light shade. Cannot be raised true from seed, so divide in late spring or early summer after flowering has finished.

Hemerocallis 'Starling' (daylily) **3–9**
Size: 3 x 2 ft. (90 x 60 cm)
Description: Purple-brown lily-like flowers, each lasting for only a day, above a clump of strap-like foliage from midsummer until late autumn.
Cultivation: Daylilies are tough plants but they respond best to well-drained, fertile soil in full sun. Split plants every three years or so.

Iris 'Wild Ginger' **4–9**
Size: 3 x 2 ft. (90 x 60 cm)
Description: A warm brown flower with white markings on the lower petals, blooming in early summer.
Cultivation: Plant the rhizomes in well-drained fertile soil in full sun, leaving the upper part of the rhizome exposed. Tolerant of drought. Lift and divide every few years to rejuvenate old plants.

Rudbeckia hirta 'Nutmeg' **annual**
Size: up to 3 x 2 ft. (90 x 60 cm)
Description: Daisy-like, russet orange flowers with a dark cone-shaped center, produced from late summer to fall.
Cultivation: Prefers heavy, moist soil and will tolerate some degree of shade. Although perennial under some circumstances, it tends to be short-lived and is not reliably hardy. Best grown as an annual or biennial.

Verbascum 'Helen Johnson' (mullein) **6–9**
Size: 3 x 1 ft. (90 x 30 cm)
Description: Tall gray spires with peachy caramel flowers above a rosette of felted gray-green leaves.
Cultivation: Short-lived perennial, perhaps best treated as biennial. Needs well-drained, preferably limy, soil and does well in full sun. Tolerant of drought and poor soil conditions.

Black

Cornus alba 'Kesselringii'
(Tatarian dogwood) **2–7**
Size: 6 x 6 ft. (1.8 x 1.8 m)
Description: Vigorous deciduous shrub. The flowers, produced in late spring, are cream. The new young leaves open russet brown and turn purple before falling in autumn, leaving the dark purple-black stems naked all winter.

Cultivation: Tolerant of most soil conditions, although it prefers a high level of fertility. Best grown in full sun. Cut back to the ground every other early spring to promote the growth of new, richly colored stems.

Iris 'Black Knight' **4–9**
Size: 3 x 2 ft. (90 x 60 cm)
Description: Black-purple flowers borne in early summer above a fan of sword-shaped leaves.
Cultivation: Plant the rhizomes in well-drained fertile soil in full sun, leaving the upper part of the rhizome exposed. Tolerant of drought. Lift and divide every few years to rejuvenate old plants.

Ophiopogon planiscapus 'Nigrescens' **6–9**
Size: 8 x 12 in. (20 x 30 cm)
Description: Clumps of leaves like black grass, with lilac, bell-like flowers hanging from arching stems in midsummer.
Cultivation: Prefers rich, slightly acid soil, but otherwise not too fussy about position. Divide in spring to increase and rejuvenate old plants.

Phyllostachys nigra (black bamboo) **7–10**
Size: 10–15 ft. x 10–12 ft. (3–4.5 m x 3–3.7 m)
Description: Gracefully arching stems form a clump of black canes which achieve their darkest colors in a warm sunny spot.
Cultivation: Completely hardy within its zones, but best sheltered from cold wind.

Viola 'Penny Black' **annual**
Size: 9 x 12 in. (23 x 30 cm)
Description: Black-purple flowers from spring to autumn above tufts of oval leaves.
Cultivation: Perennial, often grown as annual or biennnial. This pansy comes true from seed and likes moist humus-rich soil. Cut back flower stems hard after flowering to promote repeat growth.

White

Chrysanthemum 'Pavilion',
syn. *Dendranthema* 'Pavilion' **4–8**
Size: 4 x 2½ ft. (1.2 m x 75 cm)
Description: Herbaceous perennial. A florist's chrysanthemum with incurved, spherical, snow-white flowerheads.

Cultivation: In areas with mild winters can be left in ground, but in colder areas must be lifted after flowering and stored in sand or potting mix in a frost-free spot.

Cosmos bipinnatus 'White Sensation' **annual**
Size: 4 x 2 ft. (1.2m x 60 cm)
Description: Half-hardy annual with single flower heads.
Cultivation: Needs moist but well-drained soil in full sun. Grow from seed in spring and plant out when frosts are over. Flowers throughout the summer.

Lupinus 'Noble Maiden'
4–6; further south, treat as annual
Size: 3 x 2½ ft. (90 x 75 cm)
Description: Clump-forming perennial with spikes of creamy white flowers.
Cultivation: Lupines dislike limy, wet soil. Best grown as biennials, sowing seed in late spring and planting out in late summer, to flower the following season.

Rosa 'Alba Semiplena' **3–9**
Size: 8 x 5 ft. (2.5 x 1.5 m)
Description: A very old rose with semi-double flowers, delicate, exquisite scent and wonderful matte gray-green leaves. Superb in a large border or wild garden.
Cultivation: A tough plant, this will survive poor soils and some shade.

Rosa 'Blanche Double de Coubert' **3–9**
Size: 5 x 4 ft. (1.5 x 1.2 m)
Description: A rugosa hybrid, this has almost the best white flowers of any white rose and has a superb scent. Rich dark green crinkled foliage.
Cultivation: All rugosa roses are tough and adaptable to a variety of conditions, and this is no exception. Makes a good informal hedge as well as adapting well to a container. One of the very few essential garden plants.

Rosa 'Iceberg' **5–9**
Size: 4 x 2 ft. (1.2 m x 60 cm)
Description: A wonderfully clear and pure floribunda that flowers continuously from early summer to Christmas, depending on your region.
Cultivation: Prefers a deep, fertile soil. Needs full sun. Cut back old growth each early spring to maintain a good shape and encourage new flowering shoots.

Pink

Papaver orientale 'Mrs. Perry'
(Oriental poppy) **3–8**
Size: 3 × 3 ft. (90 × 90 cm)
Description: A hardy perennial, with a clump of hairy, finely divided foliage from which sprout crumpled flowers of a refined peachy pink.
Cultivation: Any good garden soil in full sun. Dies back after flowering and is best moved or divided in autumn. In flower, the stems may need support.

Rosa 'Albertine' **4–9**
Size: 20 × 12 ft. (6 × 3.7 m) or more
Description: One of the least rampant ramblers with distinctive salmon-colored buds opening into pink, slightly shaggy flowers. New leaves are bronze. Stiff stems with sharp spikes.
Cultivation: Has the vigor of all the rambler roses, but if trained it will cover a low wall or hedge, or climb a small tree. Prone to mildew.

Rosa 'Great Maiden's Blush',
syn. *R.* 'Cuisse de Nymphe' **3–9**
Size: 5 × 4 ft. (1.5 × 1.2 m)
Description: One of the most exquisite flowers on Earth, with fully double, pinkish-white blooms produced in early and midsummer. Very fragrant.
Cultivation: Like all albas, it is tough and undemanding. Prune back lightly in early spring.

Rosa 'New Dawn' **4–9**
Size: 10 × 15 ft. (3 × 4.5 m)
Description: A modern climbing rose with fragrant, delicate pearl pink blooms, borne continuously throughout summer and into autumn.
Cultivation: 'New Dawn' needs no special care. It will flower well on a west-facing wall, but prefers as much sun as possible.

Rosa 'Souvenir de la Malmaison' **5–6**
Size: 5 × 5 ft. (1.5 × 1.5 m)
Description: A Bourbon with beautifully arranged pale pink petals on continuously produced flowers. Wonderful spicy scent. Habit of growth is dense and spreading. Has a climbing sport.
Cultivation: There is no secret to growing roses: rich soil, good drainage, a thick mulch every spring, and a continuous supply of water will always do the trick.

Red

Beta vulgaris (ruby chard) **annual**
Size: 2 × 1 ft. (60 × 30 cm)
Description: Bright scarlet stems with floppy spinach-like dark green leaves, purplish when young.
Cultivation: Sow in rows in spring, and thin seedlings to 6 in. (15 cm) spacing. Keep moist to prevent running to seed.

Cotinus 'Flame' (smoke bush) **4–8**
Size: 20 × 15 ft. (6 × 4.5 m)
Description: A large bush grown entirely for its autumnal color which is exceptionally vivid.
Cultivation: Hardy and happy in any reasonable soil or position, but produces best color in an open sunny spot. Do not enrich the soil too much as this will reduce the quality of the autumn color.

Crocosmia 'Lucifer' **5–9**
Size: 3 × 1 ft. (90 × 30 cm)
Description: Branches of arching stems with vivid vermilion flowers in midsummer, between long pleated leaves.
Cultivation: Tough but not always 100 percent hardy—may benefit from some winter protection. Provide well-drained soil and plenty of sunshine.

Dahlia 'Bishop of Llandaff' **7–9**
Size: 3 × 1½ ft. (90 × 45 cm)
Description: Brilliant red flowers, contrasting with purple foliage and stems.
Cultivation: Dahlias are frost tender so their tubers should either be dug up after flowering and stored in a dry frostfree place until the following spring, or planted sufficiently deep and given a protective mulch against freezing.

Lychnis chalcedonica (Jerusalem cross) **4–8**
Size: 3 × 1 ft. (90 × 30 cm)
Description: Bright red umbels of midsummer flowers on hairy stems.
Cultivation: Well-drained soil in sun.

Phaseolus coccineus (green bean) **annual**
Size: 8 × 1 ft. (2.5 m × 30 cm)
Description: Annual climber with scarlet flowers preceding the familiar seed pods.
Cultivation: Needs heat, moisture, and shade. Best sown indoors and planted out after all frost has passed. Enrich the soil with manure and moisture-retentive organic material well before planting. Drench once a week rather than spraying daily. Support with canes or beansticks.

Quercus coccinea (scarlet oak) **5–9**
Size: 80 × 30 ft. (25 × 9 m)
Description: Superb oak tree, with deeply lobed green leaves turning bright red in autumn.
Cultivation: Hardy, but needs an acidic soil. The best autumn colors are found in the areas with the hottest summers.

Rosa 'Souvenir du Docteur Jamain' **4–9**
Size: up to 10 ft. (3 m)
Description: A hybrid perpetual with deeply maroon, velvety flowers produced from midsummer through to winter. Beautifully fragrant.
Cultivation: Particularly precious for its ability to flourish in partial shade. Hot sun spoils it, but beware of it drying out if planted against an east or north wall.

Orange

Calendula officinalis 'Orange King'
(pot-marigold) **annual**
Size: 1½ × 1 ft. (45 × 30 cm)
Description: Bright orange daisy-like flowers, good for cutting, and a brilliant contrast in a blue border. Aromatic leaves. Exceptionally useful as autumn color.
Cultivation: A hardy annual. Sow seeds where they are to flower in spring or autumn. Needs well-drained soil.

Cucurbita maxima 'Etampes' (pumpkin) **annual**
Size: 4 × 4 ft. (1.2 × 1.2 m)
Description: A bright orange-skinned, old French variety, but there are many others to choose from. The young green shoots are delicious as a vegetable.
Cultivation: A tender annual, sow seed indoors in individual pots in mid-spring, or else wait until after frosts have passed and sow directly in the soil, allowing at least 4 ft. (1.2 m) for the plant to spread. Greedy and thirsty, so add any amount of manure and keep well-watered in dry spells, especially when the fruits are beginning to swell.

Eschscholzia californica
(California poppy) **annual**
Size: 12 × 6 in. (30 × 15 cm)
Description: A hardy annual with bright orange, poppy-like flowers and fine ferny foliage. Good for cutting.
Cultivation: Sow seeds where they are to flower. Will thrive on very poor, well-drained soil, but must have sunshine.

Geum 'Borisii' **4–8**
Size: 1½ × 1 ft. (45 × 30 cm)
Description: Hardy, clump-forming perennial with deep orange petals and yellow stamens. Flowers from late spring until late summer.
Cultivation: Needs full sun and a well-drained soil that does not dry out—add plenty of organic matter to maintain moisture levels.

Kniphofia 'Prince Igor' (red-hot poker) **7–9**
Size: 6 × 6 ft. (1.8 × 1.8 m)
Description: Clumps of strap-shaped leaves, with eponymous reddish-orange flower spikes appearing in late summer and autumn.
Cultivation: Needs rich, but well-drained soil. Should be hardy, but in colder districts cover the crown with a winter mulch to protect from excessive frost.

Rudbeckia hirta 'Marmalade' or 'Rustic Dwarfs' (black-eyed Susan) **annual**
Size: 1–3 ft. × 1–1½ ft. (30–90 cm × 30–45 cm)
Description: Orange-bronze daisy-like flowers with a conical dark brown center, and lance-shaped green leaves. Flowers from summer through to autumn.
Cultivation: Sow seed in late spring, or divide plants in autumn or spring. A short-lived perennial raised as an annual or biennial. Happy on fairly heavy soil, in sun or light shade, but needs to have good drainage.

Tagetes patula (French marigold) **annual**
Size: 9 × 12 in. (23 × 30 cm)
Description: A compact plant, with masses of either single or double flowerheads, and delicate, deeply divided leaves.
Cultivation: Tagetes is a half-hardy annual, so sow seed indoors. Plant out after all risk of frost has passed, in full sun and a well-drained, reasonably fertile soil. Dead-heading prolongs the display. Good for cutting.

Yellow

Clematis 'Bill Mackenzie' **3–9**
Size: 20 × 10 ft. (6 × 3 m)
Description: A vigorous climber with small bell-shaped flowerheads appearing in late summer—lasting to Christmas if planted in a sheltered site—followed by silvery, fluffy seedheads.

Cultivation: Prune back to 1 ft. (30 cm) in early spring to encourage new growth, which will flower later in summer. Plant deeply and keep well watered.

Crocus x *luteus* 'Golden Yellow' syn. *Crocus* 'Dutch Yellow' **3–8**
Size: 4 x 3 in. (10 x 8 cm)
Description: Each bulb can have three to five pure yellow flowers in early spring.
Cultivation: Fully hardy bulb, naturalizing easily in sunny, well-drained situations.

Eranthis hyemalis (winter aconite) **5–8**
Size: 2 x 4 in. (5 x 10 cm)
Description: Often the first flower of the year, making bright yellow clumps with green ruffs, appearing in late winter and early spring.
Cultivation: Likes moist, cool conditions but only flowers in sunlight. Best planted or moved while still in flower.

Helianthus annuus (sunflower) **annual**
Size: 10 ft. (3 m) plus
Description: The most dramatic of all garden plants. Gloriously optimistic flowerheads on towering stems with huge plates of seeds after flowering.
Cultivation: A hardy annual, easily grown from the large seeds. Can be started off in individual pots indoors, or planted directly in spring. They may require staking.

Ilex aquifolium 'Bacciflava' (English holly) **7–9**
Size: 40 x 20 ft. (12 x 6 m)
Description: Dark green, prickly leaved female holly which produces bright yellow berries in winter.
Cultivation: See entry for *Ilex aquifolium* under SIGHT (pages 148–149).

Iris pseudacorus (yellow flag iris) **5–9**
Size: 5 x 5 ft. (1.5 x 1.5 m)
Description: Large yellow flowers with delicate petals and ribbed grayish-green upright leaves.
Cultivation: Grows vigorously in wet, boggy conditions.

Ligularia przewalskii **4–8**
Size: 5 x 3 ft. (1.5m x 90 cm)
Description: Black stems rise out of deeply cut leaves and bear long slender racemes of yellow flowers.
Cultivation: All ligularias like to have moist roots so are ideal for heavy soils and bog gardens. Add extra manure and protect from too much wind or sun.

Primula vulgaris (English primrose) **5–9**
Size: 6 x 6 in. (15 x 15 cm)
Description: My favorite spring flower, with delicate pale yellow petals borne on stems that grow out from a rosette of spatulate leaves.
Cultivation: Primroses are plants of deciduous woodland and thrive in the light shade and rich soil of that environment. They love limy soil.

Trollius europaeus (globe flower) **3–7**
Size: 2 x 1½ ft. (60 x 45 cm)
Description: Bears goblet-shaped flowers resembling giant buttercups.
Cultivation: It only grows in moist soil and is ideal for the edge of a pool.

Green

Galtonia viridiflora (summer hyacinth)
Size: 36 x 9 in. (90 x 23 cm)
Description: A bulb that produces strap-shaped, fleshy, gray-green leaves and, in summer, a spike with hanging bells of greenish-white flowers.
Cultivation: Not reliably hardy; either pot up to overwinter indoors, or protect with a thick mulch, depending upon your conditions. Needs rich, well-drained soil and a sunny position.

Helleborus argutifolius, syn. *H. corsicus* (Corsican hellebore) **6–8**
Size: 3 x 3 ft. (90 x 90 cm)
Description: Leathery green leaves with serrated edges, topped with pale green flower cups in late winter and early spring.
Cultivation: In the wild it will grow in very dry shade but is best in rich soil and full sun. Seeds itself readily. Cut flowering stems to the ground in summer.

Helleborus viridis (green hellebore) **6–8**
Size: 1 x 1 ft. (30 x 30 cm)
Description: Dark green divided leaves, with lime-green flowers in late winter and early spring.
Cultivation: Good in a woodland, where the shade from a deciduous tree canopy will suit it. Cut off old leaves when the new foliage and flowers appear.

Moluccella laevis (bells of Ireland) **annual**
Size: 24 x 8 in. (60 x 20 cm)
Description: The actual flowers are tiny and white, but each is cupped by a large, shell-like, pale green calyx which amounts to the "flower."

Cultivation: A tender annual that is best sown in seed trays, pricked out, and then transplanted to final position. Can be slow to germinate, but tough and long-flowering once planted.

Nicotiana langsdorffii (flowering tobacco) **annual**
Size: 4 x 1 ft. (1.2 m x 30 cm)
Description: Branching stems above oval leaves with hanging, tubular flowers of pale yellowish-green in summer.
Cultivation: Tender perennial grown as an annual. Start sowing in spring, in heated conditions indoors, and plant out when risk of frost has passed.

Tulipa 'Spring Green' **grown as annual**
Size: 15 x 6 in. (40 x 15 cm)
Description: The fundamentally white petals have a green flush. Very good gray-green leaves. Flowers in late spring.
Cultivation: Plant bulbs 6 in. (15 cm) deep in well-drained soil. Drainage is everything to a tulip, so add extra pea gravel if your soil is at all heavy.

Zinnia 'Envy' **annual**
Size: 2 x 1 ft. (60 x 30 cm)
Description: Double daisy-like flowers with quilled petals, in a pale green.
Cultivation: A tender annual, best started off early indoors, and planted out to flower when frosts have passed. Needs all the sunshine it can get.

Blue

Anchusa azurea 'Loddon Royalist' **3–8**
Size: 4 x 2 ft. (1.2 m x 60 cm)
Description: An herbaceous perennial with single flowers on spikes that are held well above the coarse hairy leaves in a brilliant jewel-like shade of blue. Flowers in early summer.
Cultivation: It must have good drainage; otherwise it may not survive a wet winter.

Brachyscombe iberidifolia (Swan River daisy) **annual**
Size: 1½ x 1½ ft. (45 x 45 cm)
Description: Lots of small daisy-like flowers in mauve-blue with yellow centers.
Cultivation: Must have sunshine and a humus-rich soil. Pinch back the tips of young growth to encourage the plant to become bushy. Can be grown from seed: either sown indoors early or where it is to flower, later in spring.

Centaurea cyanus (cornflower) **annual**
Size: 3 x 1 ft. (90 x 30 cm)
Description: Gray-green leaves and branching stems with double daisy-like sky blue flowers in summer.
Cultivation: An easy, fast-growing annual, which can be sown directly in the ground where it is to flower. It will grow in poor conditions, but responds well to rich soil. Prefers a sunny spot.

Delphinium elatum hybrids **3–9**
Size: up to 7 ft. (2.2m)
Description: Delphiniums as they ought to be: towering spires of the purest blue borne in summer.
Cultivation: Some varieties can be grown from seed—they may flower in the same year if sown early enough indoors. Give a position in full sun, and well-drained but rich soil. Stake the flowers early *before* they need it.

Hosta sieboldiana var. *elegans* **3–9**
Size: 3 x 5 ft. (90 cm x 1.5 m)
Description: Large, heart-shaped, ribbed, steely blue-green leaves with small trumpet-shaped pale lilac flowers produced in early summer.
Cultivation: Although quite tolerant of bright sunshine, the best leaf color is held in cool shade. Hostas need winter wet to do well and are best in distinctly moist conditions. Slugs and snails are a menace, and it is advisable to mulch with gravel as a deterrent.

Meconopsis betonicifolia **6–8**
Size: 3 x 1½ ft. (90 x 45 cm)
Description: The iciest of all blue plants with poppy-like flowers carried above hairy leaves.
Cultivation: Quite a fussy plant, it needs an acidic soil, plenty of humus (leaf mold is ideal), moisture, and some shade. Can be grown from freshly collected seed.

Myosotidium hortensia (Chatham Island forget-me-not) **7–9**
Size: 2 x 2 ft. (60 x 60 cm)
Description: Large glossy leaves, deeply ribbed, and clusters of forget-me-not-like flowers in a deep bright blue.
Cultivation: One of the more difficult plants to grow. It needs lots of moisture, but good drainage. It wants sunshine, but not heat, and some shade. It must be kept cool, but is not frost hardy and hates wind. Deterred? One glimpse of the flowers makes the challenge worthwhile.

Purple

Allium hollandicum 'Purple Sensation'
syn. *A. afflatunense* 'Purple Sensation' **4–8**
Size: 30 x 6 in. (75 x 15 cm)
Description: Round pompoms, like
lollipops, on tall stems.
Cultivation: They are a bulbous hardy
perennial, doing best in full sun and with
good drainage.

Buddleia davidii **5–9**
Size: 15 x 10 ft. (4.5 x 3m)
Description: One of the most familiar of
all garden plants with curving panicles of
purple flowers borne in late summer, and
toothed leaves.
Cultivation: Although they will grow in
brick walls, buddleias perform best in full
sun and rich soil. Flowers on current
season's growth, so prune very hard early
each spring.

Clematis 'Polish Spirit' **3–9**
Size: 10 x 3 ft. (3m x 90 cm)
Description: Climber with large purple
flowers produced in late summer through
to frosts of autumn.
Cultivation: Prune back to 12 in. (30 cm)
in late winter as all flowers are produced
on current growth. Plant deeply, and keep
roots cool and moist.

Cotinus coggygria 'Royal Purple' **4–8**
Size: 18 x 15 ft. (5.5 x 4.5 m)
Description: Deciduous shrub with
rounded purple leaves and a haze of pink
flowers in summer.
Cultivation: Best used as a foil at the
back of a border. Prune to encourage new
growth, which is intensely colored. Do
not overfeed.

Iris 'Dusky Challenger' **4–9**
Size: 3 x 2 ft. (90 x 60 cm)
Description: Has silky, ruffled flowers
with deep violet beard.
Cultivation: Plant the rhizome so the
top is above the surface of the soil, and
make sure it is not shaded after flowering
as it needs to bake in the summer.

Lavatera mauritanica (purple mallow)
annual
Size: 5 x 4 ft. (1.5 x 1.2 m)
Description: An unusual annual mallow
with deep purple, lilac-veined flowers.
Very long lasting.
Cultivation: Plant in ordinary soil. Self-
seeds everywhere.

Ocimum basilicum 'Purpurascens'
(purple basil) **annual**
Size: 12 x 8 in. (30 x 20 cm)
Description: Bronzy purple leaves and
lilac flowers.
Cultivation: Sow in pots in early spring
and watch for damping off. Plant out
when all frost has finished in the sunniest
site available.

Salvia x *superba*, syn. *S. nemorosa*
'Superba' **5–9**
Size: 3 x 3 ft. (90 x 90 cm)
Description: Has a stiff, upright habit and
flower spikes on tall stems which will
remain all summer.
Cultivation: Tolerates poor soil and
drought.

Tulipa 'Queen of the Night'
best grown as annual
Size: 2 ft. (60 cm)
Description: Deep purple flowerheads
with the silken sheen of a racehorse in
perfect condition.
Cultivation: Plant at least 6 in. (15 cm)
deep in late autumn with plenty of
drainage. Treated as an annual, or dig up
after leaves have died down and store in a
frost-free place when completely dry.

Verbena bonariensis **7–9**
Size: 6 x 1 ft. (1.8 m x 30 cm)
Description: Stiff branching stems with
curious square section carry small but
powerful and long-lasting purple flowers
in late summer and autumn.
Cultivation: Direct sow in spring in full
sun. Plants often die in hard winters but
self-sow very freely.

Magenta

Cosmos bipinnatus 'Sensation' **annual**
Size: 3 x 2 ft. (90 x 60 cm)
Description: An annual with beautiful
bushes of feathery delicate foliage topped
by flowers, like large saucers of brilliant
pink, with yellow eye.
Cultivation: Sow seed indoors in spring
and plant out when the danger of frost is
past. Needs plenty of sunshine and a
moisture-retentive, but not boggy, soil.

Geranium psilostemon **4–8**
Size: 4 x 4 ft. (1.2 x 1.2 m)
Description: The violently pink flowers
hover on fine stems above a mound of
finely cut leaves.

Cultivation: Quite happy with cool moist
conditions, but generally unfussy. Tolerates
some shade, but prefers sun.

Lychnis coronaria (rose campion) **4–8**
Size: 2 x 1½ ft. (60 x 45 cm)
Description: Gray hairy leaves form
clumps, from which emerge strongly
branching stems topped with magenta
flowers in early summer.
Cultivation: A short-lived perennial, it is
often grown as a biennial—sown in one
season to flower the next. Will tolerate
quite poor, dry conditions.

Rhododendron 'Hatsugiri' **6–9**
Size: 3 x 3 ft. (90 x 90 cm)
Description: A dwarf evergreen azalea
reliably smothered in small bright
magenta flowers in spring. Rare.
Cultivation: Needs acidic soil and is small
enough to be grown in a pot if ground
conditions are unsuitable. Must have good
drainage, but not be allowed to dry out at
the roots either. Tolerates light shade.

Rosa 'Gypsy Boy', syn.
R. 'Zigeunerknabe' **5–9**
Size: 5 x 5 ft. (1.5 x 1.5 m)
Description: Double flowers shade to
almost purple-black with primrose yellow
anthers. A vigorous rose with coarse leaves
and slightly floppy habits, it can be tied in
to climb. One good flush of rosettes in
summer. No scent.
Cultivation: 'Gypsy Boy' will grow and
flower in shade, which makes it an
extremely useful rose.

Rosa 'Rose de Rescht' **4–9**
Size: 3 x 3 ft. (90 x 90 cm)
Description: The almost pompom
flowers of rather smoky magenta have a
wonderful scent. Blooms consistently
through the summer.
Cultivation: For the first five years it
needs no attention beyond that dictated
by common sense but, to maintain free
flowering, prune hard as it ages.

Rosa rugosa **3–9**
Size: 5 x 3 ft. (1.5 m x 90 cm)
Description: A very vigorous healthy
species rose with prickly stems, wrinkled
leaves, and a succession of fragrant purple-
pink single blooms throughout summer.
Makes a quick-growing informal hedge,
and is particularly suitable for seaside areas
as it tolerates salt winds. Bulbous red hips
stay on the bushes until eaten by birds.

Cultivation: Much tougher and more
tolerant than hybrid roses, it will grow
almost anywhere.

SOUND

Bambusa multiplex, syn. *B. glaucescens*
(bamboo) **8–10**
Size: Can grow to 50 ft. (15m), but will
be very much less in a container.
Description: Evergreen and clump
forming, it is fast growing and works well
as a sibilant windbreak.
Cultivation: Likes moist, rich soil. Will
tolerate some shade. Propagate by dividing
clumps in spring.

Cortaderia selloana (pampas
grass) **7–10**
Size: 10 x 5 ft. (3 x 1.5 m)
Description: The familiar Pampas grass
of so many gardens has a shaggy base of
slender, arching (and very sharp) leaves
topped by great feathery wands, which
sway in the wind.
Cultivation: It needs as sunny a site as
possible and good drainage. Protect the
crowns of young plants in winter and cut
back old growth in early spring.

Glyceria maxima 'Variegata' **5–9**
Size: 3 ft. (90 cm) x indefinite spread
Description: A pretty grass striped with
yellowish cream.
Cultivation: It grows easily in cultivated
ground but it can be *very* invasive once
established, so do not grow in a mixed
border. Ideal for a rougher area of the
garden or a container. Cut back last year's
dead foliage in early spring.

Hordeum jubatum (squirreltail grass) **5–9**
Size: will grow to 2 x 1 ft. (60 x 30 cm)
Description: A form of barley and shares
the commercial crop's silky brush on a
straight stem which swishes in the wind.
Cultivation: Needs well-drained soil in a
sunny position.

Lunaria annua (honesty) **annual**
Size: 3 x 1 ft. (90 x 30 cm)
Description: Although honesty has
flowers that range from white through to
pale purple via rather a pungent violet, it
is grown for its distinctive, disk-like
translucent seed heads.
Cultivation: It is an annual that should be
sown in early summer. Self seeds easily.

Miscanthus sinensis **4–9**
Size: 12 × 4 ft. (3.7 × 1.2 m)
Description: A deciduous grass, forming clumps of tall, blue-green spikes topped with surprised-looking silky heads.
Cultivation: Grows in any cultivated soil but dislikes sitting in cold, wet ground.

Molinia caerulea (moor grass) **4–8**
Size: 5 ft. × 6 in. (1.5 m × 15 cm)
Description: A very densely tufted grass with delicate panicles about 3 ft. (90 cm) high that grow up high above the leaves.
Cultivation: Originates from damp moorland so grow in well-drained but moist position. Does not like alkaline soil.

Papaver somniferum 'Peony Flowered' (opium poppy) **8–10 (further north treat as annual)**
Size: 4 × 1 ft. (1.2 m × 30 cm)
Description: Few plants are so satisfying in all their stages as this poppy. It develops beautifully fluffy flowers ranging from pink to deep maroon-purple followed by large glaucous seedheads which then dry out to a brittle skull, rattling in the wind.
Cultivation: Poppies like recently cultivated soil, so sow the seeds in situ, scattering them and raking them well in. Thin seedlings as they appear.

TASTE

Sweet

Ficus carica (fig) **7–10**
Size: 30 × 20 ft. (15 × 6 m)
(will prune back to 6 × 6 ft. (1.8 × 1.8 m))
Description: Huge, instantly identifiable lobed leaves on sparse woody growth.
Cultivation: In a cool climate figs need a sheltered sunny wall for protection from frost. The best fruit is obtained from trees grown in distinctly poor, stony soil.

Fragaria alpina 'Semperflorens', syn. *F. vesca* (alpine strawberry) **5–9**
Size: 6 × 6 in. (15 × 15 cm)
Description: Tiny berry-sized fruit on delicate plants.
Cultivation: Grow from seed, either sowing in heat indoors in late winter to mid-spring for planting out 18 in. (30 cm) apart in a sunny situation in mid-spring to early summer. Although they do not spread from runners, the plants can be divided every few years.

Malus domestica 'Cox's Orange Pippin' (apple) **5–8**
Size: 3 ft. (90 cm) to 33 ft. (10m), depending upon rootstock and training
Description: Makes rather a scraggy tree.
Cultivation: Cox are notoriously tricky to grow well. They hate being too wet and yet must have adequate moisture, and they need a warm, sunny spot sheltered from cold winds. They must be grown in pairs to ensure pollination and often only crop biennally. However, worth the trouble if you have the right conditions.

Pastinaca sativa (parsnip) **annual**
Size: 2 × 1 ft. (60 × 30 cm) above ground: up to 2 ft. (60 cm) below ground
Description: Leafy top with single conical root.
Cultivation: Sow them shallowly from early to late spring, 3–4 in. (8–10 cm) apart, thinning out when they germinate, and harvesting them from mid-autumn onward throughout the winter. Impervious to frost, they can be left in the ground and dug as required.

Pisum sativum (pea) **annual**
Size: height depends on variety—1½ to 7 ft. (45 cm to 2.2 m)
Description: Self-supporting climbing legume with twining tendrils.
Cultivation: Sow from early spring to midsummer in rich soil, planting the seeds about 2 in. (5 cm) deep, 3 in. (8 cm) apart in a double row. Provide netting or sticks for support as soon as the plants emerge. Keep picking regularly.

Prunus domestica 'Greengage' (greengage) **6–8**
Size: 20 × 15 ft. (6 × 4.5 m)
Description: Typically plum-like tree with massed, spindly branches.
Cultivation: Greengages need warmth and shelter to protect the early spring blossom from frosts. The soil needs to be free-draining and preferably slightly acid. Plant new trees in late autumn to early winter, while the soil is still warm, and prune only in summer.

Prunus persica (peach) **6–9**
Size: 15 × 6 ft. (4.5 × 1.8 m)
Description: Small tree with pointed leaves. Can be pruned or fan-trained to grow against a wall.
Cultivation: Peaches prefer a slightly acid, well-drained soil, with plenty of moisture and as much sun as possible.

Pyrus communis (pear) **5–8**
Size: 50 × 20 ft. (15 × 6 m) down to 6 × 6 ft. (1.8 × 1.8 m).
Description: Makes superb pyramidal tree as well as training as cordon or espalier. Exquisite blossom in early spring and often develops good autumn leaf color.
Cultivation: Pears tolerate wetter, colder conditions than apples but still prefer a sunny site. Add manure initially but do not over-feed as this will produce more tree and less fruit. Harvest just before the fruits ripen.

Rubus idaeus (raspberry) **3–8**
Size: 6 × 1 ft. (1.8m × 30 cm)
Description: Vigorous, deciduous cane fruit with small leaves.
Cultivation: Raspberries like cool, moist soil containing plenty of organic matter. Plant canes 1½ ft. (45 cm) apart in deeply prepared trenches in early winter to early spring. Cut new canes back to 12 in. (30 cm) above soil to prevent fruiting in first year. During the next growing season tie canes to wire support. Mulch thickly every spring.

Solanum tuberosum (new potatoes) **annual**
Size: 2 × 2 ft. (60 × 60 cm)
Description: Leafy topgrowth with small white flowers.
Cultivation: Plant 1 ft. (30 cm) apart, with 1½ ft. (45 cm) between rows. All potatoes like highly fertile, well-drained, soil with lots of organic matter. Earth up as the plants grow to protect the developing tubers from the light and frost damage. Harvest when the plants begin to flower—about 75 days from planting.

Bitter

Cichorium endiva (chicory) **annual or biennial**
Size: 1 × 2 ft. (30 × 60 cm)
Description: Leafy salad vegetable available in a variety of leaf shapes and colors, including red-foliaged types.
Cultivation: Sow from early spring to midsummer for continuity. May need blanching by tying up the leaves or covering, though some may be cut straight from the garden.

Cichorium intybus (endive) **3–10**
Size: 1 × 1 ft. (30 × 30 cm)
Description: Leafy vegetable grown to force in darkness for blanched "chicons."

Cultivation: Sow in late spring or early summer. Needs deep, well-drained soil, on sand or chalk. From late autumn dig up a few roots at a time for forcing. Cut off top growth leaving about ¾in. (2 cm), plant in a pot, and keep warm and dark. Ready in about three weeks.

Rumex acetosa (large-leaved sorrel) **4–8**
Size: 1 × 1 ft. (30 × 30 cm)
Description: Dock-like leaves growing from base of plant.
Cultivation: Grows best in cool, moist conditions. Either sow seed in spring, or divide existing plants in spring or autumn. Protect with cold frame for a winter crop. Remove flower spikes as they appear to prolong leaf production.

Rumex scutatus (French sorrel) **4–8**
Size: 8 × 12 in. (20 × 30 cm)
Description: Has small, round leaves rather like watercress.
Cultivation: Grow from division of rooted pieces. Cultivation similar to that of large-leaved sorrel, but will tolerate hotter, drier conditions.

Sour

Citrus limon 'Meyer' (lemon) **9–11**
Size: 15 × 6 ft. (4.5 × 1.8 m)
Description: 'Meyer' is a compact, shrubby lemon with typical evergreen, glossy leaves and bright yellow fruits.
Cultivation: Hardier than most lemons, 'Meyer' is nevertheless tender and ideal for a conservatory. All citrus like warm, rich soil with lots of water but good drainage. Prune in early spring, hard to promote growth on young trees and for shape in mature specimens.

Malus domestica 'Bramley's Seedling' (apple) **5–8**
Size: 30 × 30 ft. (9 × 9 m)
Description: Makes a wide-spreading tree at maturity with huge, bright green, rather flattened apples. Produces wonderful blossom in spring. Has a very high vitamin C content.
Cultivation: Apples need plenty of sun and dry conditions. Do not enrich the soil too much but keep the base of the tree weed-free. Prune in winter, chiefly to improve ventilation, leaving lots of space in the middle of the tree. Needs a pollinator such as another Bramley, a 'Cox's Orange Pippin', or a 'James Grieve'.

Malus pumila (crab apple) **4–8**
Size: 30 x 10 ft. (9 x 3 m)
Description: Makes a smaller tree than most apples with smaller, brightly colored fruits. The blossom is earlier and fantastically beautiful.
Cultivation: A tough tree which can be grown anywhere that is not waterlogged.

Prunus cerasus 'Morello' (sour cherry) **5–8**
Size: 25 x 10 ft. (7.5 x 3 m)
Description: Similar to sweet cherry but smaller, with darker fruit.
Cultivation: Tolerates shade and can be grown against a north wall. Needs plenty of water. Prune out dead or diseased old wood in summer.

Prunus damascena (damson plum) **5–8**
Size: 15 x 10 ft. (4.5 x 3 m)
Description: A small untidy tree, often planted in hedges. Laden with masses of purple fruit from late summer.
Cultivation: Damsons tolerate colder and wetter conditions than other plums. Must be picked as soon as they ripen.

Ribes rubrum (redcurrant) **4–8**
Size: 7 x 5 ft. (2.2 x 1.5 m)
Description: Very nondescript shrub until the berries form, when it is transformed by the massed bright red currants with their particularly tart acidity.
Cultivation: Red- and whitecurrants like a cool spot in rich soil. Sun increases sweetness. Net to protect from birds, or they will invariably strip every single fruit before you pick them.

SCENT

Spring

Buddleia globosa (orange ball tree) **7–9**
Size: 15 x 15 ft. (4.5 x 4.5 m)
Description: Mainly evergreen shrub with globular orange flowerheads.
Cultivation: A little tender, so plant in a very sheltered site in full sun. Soil must be fertile but well-drained.

Choisya ternata (Mexican orange bush) **7–9**
Size: 8 x 6 ft. (2.5 x 1.8 m)
Description: Evergreen shrub with heavily scented, starry white flowers. Foliage also aromatic if crushed.
Cultivation: Tolerates heavy shade. Can be clipped hard to shape.

Clematis armandii **7–9**
Size: 20 x 10 ft. (6 x 3 m)
Description: Evergreen climber with leathery spear-shaped dark green leaves and lovely almond-scented white flowers in spring.
Cultivation: As with all clematis, plant deeply with lots of organic matter. It needs full sun and some protection from cold wind to flourish.

Clematis montana 'Odorata' **6–9**
Size: 30 x 30 ft. (9 x 9 m)
Description: Strong climber with starry, vanilla-scented flowers in spring.
Cultivation: Not fussy about situation, but plant deeply with plenty of organic matter. Does very well on limy soil. No need to prune, but if necessary do so immediately after flowering.

Crocus chrysanthus **4–9**
Size: 2 x 2 in. (5 x 5 cm)
Description: Delicately scented flowers appear from bare ground in early spring, in colors ranging from pale cream to deep purple or yellow.
Cultivation: Needs well-drained soil. Will naturalize in grass.

Erysimum cheiri, syn. *Cheiranthus cheiri* (wallflower) **biennial**
Size: 2 x 1 ft. (60 x 30 cm)
Description: Flowers in spring in range of bright colors from yellow through to dark red. Distinctive musky, smoky scent.
Cultivation: Grow as a biennial anywhere in sun, although best on limy soil. Sow in summer, and plant out in autumn.

Hyacinthoides non-scriptus (English bluebell) **4–9**
Size: 12 x 6 in. (30 x 15 cm)
Description: The strap-like leaves are followed by the familiar blue, nodding flower bells hanging from arching stems.
Cultivation: Woodland plants, which like best dappled shade in spring until the end of flowering, followed by heavier shade in summer. Once established they will colonize to the extent of becoming invasive, so the bulbs are best planted in grass or under trees. Prefers heavy soil.

Iris reticulata **5–9**
Size: 6 x 3 in. (15 x 8 cm)
Description: Deep, rich violet flowers, with orange tongue inside petal have a violet scent. They are produced among grassy leaves.

Cultivation: Must have very well-drained soil and plenty of heat and sunlight in summer, after flowering, to produce the best flowers the following year.

Jasminum x *stephanense* **7–9**
Size: 20 x 10 ft. (6 x 3 m)
Description: Very vigorous deciduous climber with pale green leaves and exotically fragrant, pink flowers.
Cultivation: Grow in full sun or partial shade in free-draining soil.

Lonicera japonica 'Halliana' **4–9** (Japanese honeysuckle)
Size: 20 x 15 ft. (6 x 4.5 m)
Description: Almost evergreen, vigorous climber with white and creamy yellow flowers from late spring into summer.
Cultivation: Any well-drained, cool soil. Responds well to plenty of organic matter at planting time. Prune in early spring.

Matthiola incana (Brompton stocks) **biennial**
Size: 3 x 1½ ft. (90 x 45 cm)
Description: Clove-scented, glaucous, lance-shaped leaves are topped in late spring by sweetly scented flowers in the full range of pastel shades.
Cultivation: It is a perennial but usually treated as a biennial. Sow and grow on in summer: in autumn plant out in good soil for flowering the following spring. The hotter the sun, the better the scent.

Narcissus jonquilla (jonquil) **4–9**
Size: 12 x 6 in. (30 x 15 cm)
Description: Hardy bulbs with familiar strap-shaped leaves and tiny sweetly scented yellow trumpeted flowerheads.
Cultivation: Will naturalize in grass in a sheltered sunny spot. Plant bulbs in late summer to twice the depth of the bulb. Very good for planting in a container.

Osmanthus x *burkwoodii* **7–9**
Size: 10 x 8 ft. (3 x 2.5 m)
Description: Evergreen shrub with shiny leaves and white flowers of exceptionally sweet scent.
Cultivation: Easy. Pop it in and grow it.

Osmanthus delavayii **7–9**
Size: 10 x 10 ft. (3 x 3 m)
Description: Slow-growing, small evergreen shrub with star-like white flowers and very small leaves
Cultivation: Unfussy; any well-drained soil in sun or part shade.

Rosa primula (incense rose) **5–8**
Size: 10 x 6 ft. (3 x 1.8 m)
Description: Very distinctive ferny foliage scented of incense, and primrose yellow flowers. One of the first roses to bloom.
Cultivation: Tough and adaptable, but responds well to good soil, regular watering, and an annual mulch.

Tulipa sylvestris **4–8**
Size: 18 x 4 in. (45 x 10 cm)
Description: Hardy bulb with yellow star-shaped blooms in mid-spring.
Cultivation: One of the few tulips that can be left reliably to naturalize and to increase in tough grass in the wilder parts of the garden. Tolerates light shade and more dampness than most tulips.

Wisteria sinensis 'Alba' **5–9**
Size: 35 x 50 ft. (10.6 x 15 m)
Description: Deciduous climber with pendant racemes of white flowers.
Cultivation: Usually trained against a wall, but will scramble into a tree. Needs sun or light shade, good drainage. Prune lightly after flowering and again in winter.

Summer

Brugmansia arborea, syn. *Datura arborea* **9–11**
Size: 12 x 8 ft. (3.7 x 2.5 m)
Description: Large, evergreen shrub with huge, trumpet-shaped, pendant flowers from late summer to early autumn.
Cultivation: Not frost hardy, so safest grown in a large pot and sheltered in winter. Likes some shade and plenty of water. Cut back hard in late winter.

Hesperis matronalis (sweet rocket) **4–9** **as a perennial**
Size: 4 x 3 ft. (1.2 m x 90 cm)
Description: Pale lilac, pink, and white flowers in early summer on a strongly branching plant, which become especially noticeably scented at night.
Cultivation: A perennial, but usually treated as a biennial. Plant out in sun or light shade, in any soil. Self-seeds freely.

Hoya carnosa (wax plant) **10–11**
Size: 20 x 5 ft. (6 x 1.5 m)
Description: Tender climber for the warm conservatory. Sweet and spicy scent from waxy white pink-centered flowers.
Cultivation: Needs acidic soil and a moist atmosphere. Can be pruned after flowering if necessary.

Lathyrus odoratus (sweet pea) **annual**
Size: 10 x 2 ft. (3 m x 60 cm)
Description: Climbing annual legume with exquisitely scented flowers ranging from pure white to deep maroon and purple. Avoid modern varieties as their scent is either faint or nonexistent.
Cultivation: Best sown in autumn under glass and left to overwinter in a cold frame or sheltered spot outside. Plant out in early spring with a wigwam of canes or netting to support. Regular picking will encourage repeated flowerings.

Lavandula angustifolia (lavender) **5–8**
Size: 3 x 4 ft. (90 cm x 1.2 m)
Description: Glaucous evergreen shrub with fine aromatic foliage and long spikes of fragrant flowers in summer.
Cultivation: Easily grown from seed. Likes sunshine and very well-drained soil. Prune immediately after flowering, being careful not to cut back into old wood.

Lilium candidum (Madonna lily) **4–9**
Size: 1.2m x 60 cm (4 x 2 ft.)
Description: Magnificent flowers, powerfully and heavenly scented, with up to 20 radiating out from each stem.
Cultivation: The bulbs need very well-drained and alkaline soil.

Matthiola bicornis (night-scented stock) **annual**
Size: 12 x 9 in. (30 x 23 cm)
Description: Gray-green leaves and lilac-pink flowers. Strong, sweet evening scent.
Cultivation: Hardy annual, sow where it is to flower either in early spring or the previous late summer.

Nicotiana sylvestris **annual**
Size: 5 x 2 ft. (1.5 m x 60 cm)
Description: A green rosette of very sticky oval leaves, above which tower musky white trumpet-shaped flowers that only smell at dusk.
Cultivation: Frost-tender perennial, best grown as a half-hardy annual. Start it from seed early indoors in heat. Needs full sun for the flowers to open fully.

Oenothera biennis (evening primrose) **biennial**
Size: 3 x 3 ft. (90 x 90 cm)
Description: Pale yellow flowers that open and release a powerful scent at dusk.
Cultivation: Can self-seed with enthusiasm, so plant in a wilder area of garden. Needs sun and well-drained soil.

Philadelphus delavayi **6–8**
Size: 10 x 6 ft. (3 x 1.8 m)
Description: Upright deciduous shrub with pure white, highly scented flowers in early summer.
Cultivation: Any soil in full sun but does best on lime.

Rosa x *centifolia* 'Cristata', syn. *R.* 'Chapeau de Napoleon' **4–9**
Size: 4 x 4 ft. (1.2 x 1.2 m)
Description: A prickly, lax-growing bush with fresh green leaves and double pink blooms. The markedly mossy buds are shaped like a tricorn hat. Clear rose scent.
Cultivation: As with all roses, a rich soil in full sun and a regular water supply will give good growth. Prune only to shape.

Rosa 'Madame Plantier' **3–9**
Size: 12 x 12 ft. (3.7 x 3.7 m)
Description: A sprawling shrub or a low climber. Strongly scented double flowers in summer—pink in bud, cream as they open, and fading to white.
Cultivation: Tolerates shade better than many roses and can be planted to climb into a tree or shrub. Prune only to shape.

Rosmarinus officinalis (rosemary) **8–10**
Size: 5 x 5 ft. (1.5 x 1.5 m)
Description: Evergreen shrub with aromatic, gray-green leaves, and white to purple-blue flowers in early summer.
Cultivation: Not fully hardy—needs a sheltered spot, maximum sun, and free-draining soil; take cuttings as a safeguard.

Syringa vulgaris 'Madame Lemoine' (lilac) **3–9**
Size: 22 x 12 ft. (6.7 x 3.7 m)
Description: Pale green heart-shaped leaves. Double white flowers with typical lilac scent in early summer.
Cultivation: Not too fussy and will tolerate light shade and all but the most limy soils. Grows back vigorously from hard pruning and, when in a border, is best cut to the ground every other year.

Autumn

Buddleia auriculata **7–9**
Size: 12 x 6 ft. (3.7 x 1.8 m)
Description: Tender evergreen shrub with thin leaves and delicate panicles of cream flowers in autumn. Rare.
Cultivation: A plant for a conservatory or sheltered south wall. Prune after flowering.

Clematis rehederiana **6–9**
Size: 25 x 8 ft. (7.5 x 2.5 m)
Description: A deciduous climber with pale yellow bell flowers in late summer and autumn. Good for growing through other plants that have finished flowering.
Cultivation: Prefers a limy soil with a cool root run. Flowers on current season's growth, so prune back to 12 in. (30 cm) in early spring.

Cosmos atrosanguineus (Chocolate cosmos) **6–9**
Size: 1 x 1½ ft. (30 x 45 cm)
Description: The very distinctive chocolate scent matches the chocolate-colored stems and the incredible richness of the crimson flowers of this lovely plant.
Cultivation: In cold areas lift the tubers in autumn; replant in spring. In warmer areas protect with a mulch in winter. Grows easily from basal cuttings taken in spring.

Hamamelis virginiana **4–8**
Size: 12 x 12 ft. (3.7 x 3.7 m)
Description: A deciduous shrub whose small yellow flowers appear as the leaves fall in autumn.
Cultivation: It needs a sheltered site with partial shade.

Lonicera periclymenum 'Graham Thomas' (honeysuckle) **5–9**
Size: 20 x 10 ft. (6 x 3 m)
Description: A variety of the common honeysuckle with pale yellow flowers appearing in late summer.
Cultivation: Whilst not fussy, all honeysuckles prefer a cool moist root run.

Winter

Chimonanthus praecox (wintersweet) **7–9**
Size: 12 x 10 ft. (3.7 x 3 m)
Description: The primrose yellow flowers that smell so delicious are produced from early winter through to early spring, before the leaves appear on this shrub.
Cultivation: Ideal for a south-facing wall.

Clematis cirrhosa var. *balearica* **7–9**
Size: 10 x 5 ft. (3 x 1.5 m)
Description: Evergreen climber producing small creamy yellow flowers spattered inside with pink from early winter through to mid-spring.
Cultivation: Give a warm, sheltered site. Plant deeply and, as with all clematis, mulch and water well.

Daphne mezereum **4–7**
Size: 4 x 2 ft. (1.2 m x 60 cm)
Description: A small, distinctly upright, deciduous shrub with a dense covering of purple flowers appearing on the bare branches just before the leaves emerge.
Cultivation: Likes cool moist conditions, best achieved with partial shade and a heavy mulch each spring.

Daphne odora **7–9**
Size: 5 x 4 ft. (1.5 x 1.2 m)
Description: Evergreen daphne with rather leathery leaves and lilac to pink flowers in late winter
Cultivation: As for *Daphne mezereum*.

Galanthus nivalis (snowdrop) **3–8**
Size: 4 x 2 in. (10 x 5 cm)
Description: Familiar white hanging bells and chalky green stems and leaves.
Cultivation: Prefers moist soil and light shade. Best planted "in the green," during or just after flowering, rather than as bulbs. Divide every three or four years.

Hamamelis mollis (witch hazel) **5–8**
Size: 12 x 12 ft. (3.7 x 3.7 m)
Description: Large deciduous shrub with extraordinary starbursts of yellow flowers from late winter into spring.
Cultivation: Prefers a slightly acidic soil, but not too fussy.

Lonicera fragrantissima (winter-flowering honeysuckle) **5–8**
Size: 6 x 10 ft. (1.8 x 3 m)
Description: Delicate white flowers are produced in midwinter on bare stems. Heavenly scent.
Cultivation: A shrub that likes to be shaded and—helpfully—will grow pretty well in dry shade.

Sarcococca humilis (Christmas box) **7–9**
Size: 2 x 3 ft. (60 x 90 cm)
Description: Small evergreen with dark shiny foliage and white flowers in late winter, tinged with pink.
Cultivation: A very obliging plant, tolerating even dry shade.

Viburnum x *bodnantense* 'Dawn' **6–8**
Size: 10 x 6 ft. (3 x 1.8 m)
Description: A medium-sized deciduous shrub producing pink globules of flower on bare branches all winter.
Cultivation: Performs best in full sun and in rich border soil. Prune for size and shape in spring, after flowering.

INDEX

Acknowledgments

The publisher would like to thank the following photographers and agencies for their kind permission to reproduce the photographs in this book:

Pages 2–3 Andrew Lawson (Monet's garden, Giverney); **6** Andrea Jones/Boxtree (Taken from *Garden Doctors* by Dan Pearson and Steve Bradley, published by Boxtree); **9** Andrea Jones; **11** Andrew Lawson; **12** *above* Anne Hyde; **12** *below* JS Sira/The Garden Picture Library; **13** Michele Lamontagne (Saiho-ji); **14** Allen Rokach; **15** Sue Snell; **16** Claire de Vireu/SIP (Jardin d'Andre Eve, Pithiviers); **17** Hugh Palmer (Oare House); **18** Sue Snell; **19** Sabine Vollmer von Falken; **20** Marijke Heuff (Nicole de Vesian); **21** *above* Annette Schreiner; **21** *below* Sunniva Harte (Merriments); **22** *below left* Clive Nichols; **22** *below right* Jean Pierre Godeaut (Bambou Anduze); **22–23** *above* F.Rozet/Image du Sud; **23** *below right* Jean Pierre Godeaut (Designer: Gilles Clement); **23** *below left* Saxon Holt; **24** John Glover (Wakehurst Place, Sussex); **26** *left* Neil Campbell-Sharp (The Courts, Wiltshire); **26** *centre and right* John Glover; **27** John Glover; **29** Lorry Eason; **1** Noel Kavanagh (10 Wildwood Road, London NW11); **32** *above* Mads Mogensen; **32** *below* Anne Hyde; **33** Marianne Majerus (Chilworth Manor, Surrey); **34** Marianne Majerus; **35** Andrew Lawson (The Priory, Charlbury, Oxfordshire); **36–37** Andrew Lawson (Gothic House, Charlbury, Oxfordshire); **38** Anne Hyde; **39** Sue Snell; **40** Richard Felber; **41** *above* Marijke Heuff (Mr & Mrs. Rutten-Yorna, Holland); **41** *centre* Gary Rogers; **41** *below* John Glover; **42** Clive Nichols; **43** *above* Dennis Davis/The Garden Picture Library; **43** *below* Marion Nickig; **44–45** Brigitte Perdereau; **46** Marianne Majerus; **47** *left* Clive Nichols; **47** *centre* Anne Hyde; **47** *right* Gary Rogers; **48** Dr Jeremy Burgess/Science Photo Library; **49** JS Sira/The Garden Picture Library; **50** *left* Richard Felber; **50** *centre* Graeme Harris/The Special Photographers Library; **50** *right* Maggie Oster (Cedar Falls); **51** *left* Photos Horticultural; **51** *centre* Maggie Oster; **51** *right* Ken Druse; **52** Harry Smith Collection; **53** Brigitte Perdereau; **54–55** Christian Sarramon; **56** John Glover; **57** *above left* Brigitte Perdereau; **57** *above right* Leigh Clapp; **57** *below* Clive Nichols; **58** *left* Clive Nichols (Sue Berger, Bristol); **58** *right* John Ferro Sims/The Garden Picture Library; **59** Clive Nichols (Southview Nurseries, Hampshire); **60** Nicola Browne (Great Dixter); **61** S & O Mathews (12 Rozelle Close); **62** *above* Sunniva Harte (Merriments); **62** *below* Andrew Lawson; **63** Brigitte Perdereau; **64** *above* Marijke Heuff; **64** *below* Andrea Jones; **65** J C Mayer–G Le Scanff ('Le Jardin de Campagne' 1995, France); **66** Brigitte Perdereau; **67** *above* Didillon/Campagne, Campagne; **67** *below* Nicola Browne (Garden Design: David Stevens); **68** *above and below* Marijke Heuff (Bingerden House, Holland); **68** *centre* Christian Sarramon; **69** *above* Marianne Majerus (Haseley Court, Oxfordshire); **69** *centre* Deidi von Schaewen; **69** *below* Marijke Heuff (Gourdon Castle Garden, France); **70–71** Claude Nuridsany & Marie Perennou/Science Photo Library; **72** Jacques Dirand/SIP (Isba de Pecheurs en Lettonie); **73** Richard Felber; **75** Claude Nuridansy & Marie Perennou/Science Photo Library; **76** *above* Clive Nichols (Kellaways Garden, Wiltshire); **76** *below* Roger Foley (Oehme); **77** Marijke Heuff (Mrs L. Goossenaerts, Holland); **78** Marijke Heuff (Patricia van Roosmalen, Belgium); **79** John Neubauer; **80** *left* Jacqui Hurst; **80** *right* Claire de Virieu/SIP; **81** Marijke Heuff (Generalife, Spain); **82–83** Anne Hyde; **84** Georges Leveque (Landscape Designer: Erwan Tymen, Brittany); **85** *left* Marijke Heuff; **85** *right* Sue Snell; **86** Stephen Dalton/Natural History Photographic Agency; **87** Arthur Morris/Windrush Photos; **88** Richard Felber; **89** Neil Campbell-Sharp; **91** Sue Snell; **92** *above* Marijke Heuff (Ineke Greve, Holland); **92** *below* Gary Rogers; **93** J C Mayer–G Le Scanff; **94** John Miller/The Garden Picture Library; **95** Juliette Wade/The Garden Picture Library; **96–97** Sue Snell; **98** *left* Howard Rice/The Garden Picture Library (Scarlett's Nursery, Colchester); **98** *right* Howard Rice/The Garden Picture Library (Wisley); **99** Clive Nichols; **100** John Glover; **101** *above* Sue Snell; **101** *below left and right* John Glover; **102** Andrew Lawson; **103** *left* Howard Rice/The Garden Picture Library (Wisley); **103** *right* Jacqui Hurst; **104** Linda Burgess/The Garden Picture Library; **105** Saxon Holt; **106** *above* Jerry Harpur; **106** *below* Mel Watson/The Garden Picture Library; **107** Michele Lamontagne/The Garden Picture Library; **108** Sue Snell; **109** *above left* Vogue Entertaining (Conde Nast Publications Ltd); **109** *above right and below* Sue Snell; **110** Sunniva Harte (Marle Place); **111** Sue Snell; **112** *above* S & O Mathews; **112** *below* Mayer–Le Scanff/The Garden Picture Library; **113** *left* Brigitte Perdereau; **113** *right* Anne Hyde; **114** Marianne Majerus (Manor Farm, Lincolnshire); **115** *above* Marijke Heuff (Mien Ruys); **115** *below* Sue Snell; **116** Marianne Majerus (Bourton House, Gloucestershire); **117** *above* Sunniva Harte (Marle Place); **117** *below* Marianne Majerus (Ballymaloe Cookery School, Co. Cork, Ireland); **119** Andrew Lawson; **120** *above* Simon Brown; **120** *below* Dr Jeremy Burgess/Science Photo Library; **121** Simon Brown; **122** S & O Mathews; **123** Jane Gifford; **124** *left* Clive Nichols; **124** *right* Frieder Blickle/Bilderberg; **125** *above* Clive Nichols (Lygon Arms, Gloucestershire); **125** *below* S & O Mathews; **126** *left* John Glover (Mannington Garden, Norfolk); **126** *right* John Glover; **127** *left* Brigitte Perdereau; **127** *right* Philippe Bonduel/The Garden Picture Library; **128** Marianne Majerus (Elsing Hall, Norfolk); **129** Jerry Harpur (Hadspen House); **130–131** S & O Mathews; **133** John Glover; **134** S & O Mathews; **135** *above* Kathy Charlton/The Garden Picture Library; **135** *below* Jane Nichols; **136–137** Bernard Limbour/SIP (Designer: Jacques Wirtz); **139** *above left* Howard Rice/The Garden Picture Library; **139** *Above right and below* Clive Nichols; **140** *left* Hugh Palmer (The Chantry, Rougham); **140** *right* Andrew Lawson; **141** *left* John Glover; **141** *right* Harry Smith Collection; **143** Claude Nuridsany & Marie Perennou/Science Photo Library; **144–145** Marijke Heuff (Garden designer: Piet Oudolf, Holland); **147** *above left* Eberhard Grames/Bilderberg; **147** *above right* Richard Felber; **147** *below* Richard Felber.

The following photographs were taken specially for Conran Octopus by Tessa Traeger: pages **4–5, 10, 30, 74, 90, 118, 140**.

The publisher would also like to thank Thea Stanton and Jane Knowles.

The quotations in the text and caption on page 89 are taken from T.S. Eliot's poem 'Burnt Norton' in *Four Quartets*, and are reproduced by kind permission of the publisher, Harcourt Brace & Company.

SIMON & SCHUSTER EDITIONS
Rockefeller Center
1230 Avenue of the Americas
New York, NY 10020

Text copyright © 1997 by Montagu Don
Design and layout copyright © 1997 by
Conran Octopus Limited

All rights reserved, including the right of
reproduction in whole or in part in any form.

SIMON & SCHUSTER EDITIONS and
colophon are trademarks of
Simon & Schuster Inc.

Designed by Leslie Harrington.

Printed in Hong Kong

10 9 8 7 6 5 4 3 2 1

Library of Congress Cataloging-in-
Publication data is available.

ISBN 0-684-83965-2